Sweating *the* Small Stuff *and loving it*

Sweating *the* Small Stuff *and loving it*

MARTY MCCRONE

echo
BOOKS

an imprint of
Wintertickle Press

Sweating
the Small
Stuff *and loving it*

Wintertickle Press
132 Commerce Park Drive
Unit K, Ste. 155
Barrie, ON L4N 0Z7
Canada

Wintericklepress.com
@wintericklepress

ISBN 978-1-989664-11-7

Dedication

For Julie, Luke, and Jake. You have endured so much and have the weight to carry throughout time. Know that I see you, understand you, and will always love you with an intensity, which may, in time, take a bit of the load off your shoulders.

CONTENTS

PROLOGUE

January 20, 2000, 3 p.m. The day my world changed. The day I would enter the strange world of Middle Earth.

After living in Baltimore and Orlando for a few years, along with dealing with a couple of cancers, we returned to Barrie Ontario, Canada. The boys were launched into their educational pursuits of medicine in universities in the US, and Julie and I were re-establishing ourselves in our home base. While Julie was re-entering the world of educational administration, I was kind of floundering. My voice was weak from the radiation, and I was unable to resume teaching. Going to the gym every morning and then ending up in Starbucks just did not fulfill me. Those hours until Julie came home loomed over me like a dark cloud. Trying to focus on cooking dinner revealed I had zero aptitude in the kitchen—Julie would attest to that! Then Julie suggested, "Why don't you write down your experiences, your anecdotes that you've been using in your talks for Gilda's Club?"

The writing experience became my therapy to the point where I actually couldn't wait to write each day. The original goal was to provide me some insight into my journey and my family's journey—as my son, Luke, said, "You didn't get cancer. The whole family got cancer." Some chapters made me laugh out loud; some brought melancholy for what I'd lost; some brought tears. It was a catharsis for sure, but I kept thinking there was something germane to the perspective I'd gained, which may be relatable to others.

Then life and new experiences took over as we forged ahead. The writings were still there but on the back burner as the merry-go-round of new opportunities were pursued. However, I decided to put my writings out there on a weekly blog called *Happy Hour with Marty*. The response was overwhelming at times, as people reached out to comment. Some people were a blast from the past from high school and even elementary school. Former students, colleagues, and friends we've made along the way reached out with messages. With difficulty, I had to answer some people who had not heard I'd had cancer and were really shocked. The C word does that to us every time!

Why publish my writings? My goal in this pursuit was a simple one—if I could positively impact even one person, on even the most infinitesimally small level, I feel like I'm paying forward the gift of my hindsight. It's why I spend hours after my wellness checkups at Princess Margaret Hospital talking to the radiation technicians.

FOREWORD

The Marty Rant

I had cancer. Period! I do not call myself a survivor. I have had many friends and acquaintances who have fought countless battles but lost the war to cancer. We all have fought hard. The fact that I lived doesn't mean I fought harder or that I had a stronger will to live. We all had excellent doctors, and all had a positive attitude. I am here because I am lucky—that's all. Lucky—perhaps the doctors caught it early. Lucky because—just because. There is no reason. Just lucky.

I have heard people talk about how they are cancer survivors, and that is the defining moment of their life. A close friend of mine said, "I am more than just the cancer."

I admit I had cancer, actually two of them. I am not all about the cancer—I am Marty. Writing this book has helped me come to that realization. It didn't start out as a book, as I was merely putting some thoughts down on paper. During the writing, I would laugh at particular situations and at other times, I would have to start a new page, as my words would be smeared beyond recognition—the page stained with tears.

The experiences in this book have been part of my journey to regain my identity and not be defined as a cancer survivor. I hope the following story will inspire the reader to understand the process that people who have been touched by cancer endure. This includes family, friends, and caregivers, as well as the warriors.

It's a beautiful day
Don't let it get away
Beautiful day
~U2

1

Another Day in Paradise

I loved my job, but not as much as the weekend and time with the family. It was finally the end of the week on a sunny Friday in November. Sunny and November are seldom said in the same sentence. I could hardly wait for the workday to end. I was going to pick up our younger son from school, and we would be on our way to Toronto to see the Toronto Raptors play basketball—a passion of mine and now a shared passion with my sons.

Life was good! I was one of those guys who knew he had it good. My best friend, Julie, had become my wife. We shared everything we did—a love of the outdoors, exercise, reading, and laughter. We met at a summer course in July in Toronto. I had just graduated from the Faculty of Education, and, of course, there were no jobs to be had anywhere. I had a chance to supply teach at an elementary school in Elmvale, Ontario. Elmvale is a very small town about an hour-and-a-half drive north of Toronto. During one of the days I was supply teaching, the principal said to me, "I like the way you are with students," and he asked me if I was qualified to teach grade five. I said, "I am only qualified to teach grade seven up to grade thirteen," (at the time, grade thirteen still existed), "but I could take a course in July to get qualified." He looked me straight in the eye, held out his hand, and we shook on the job. I couldn't believe it—I had a job! I had an old convertible MG Midget Roadster, and I remember driving the half-hour back to my house in Barrie with the tunes blaring and the wind blowing through my hair. I should have been on cloud nine that ride home, but I had to go to the house and pick up my dog of thirteen years to take him to the vet and have him put down. You see, my parents, after years after bickering and talking to one another through their kids, were separating. They couldn't, or *wouldn't*, take the dog with them to their new places, and I was renting a place that would not accept pets. Life was very unstable back then with my parents separating and selling the home I grew up in. In tears, I was putting Shep into the car when the next-door neighbour, who knew we were splitting up the home, asked what we were going to do with Shep. I explained to him the situation. Without missing a beat, he said he would take Shep. I was the happiest guy on the planet at that point! Shep, the wonder dog, would go on to live to the ripe old age of seventeen because of the kindness of a neighbour. Now I could concentrate on taking a summer course to get my first real job.

I had finished a year at the Faculty of Education and was looking forward to spending a summer in the city with my Auntie Ev and Uncle Ed, salt-of-the-earth people, who absolutely loved me unconditionally as I did them. They provided stability in my life when it was needed most. They nurtured and spoiled me every time I was around them. Living with them for my Faculty of Education year had been one of the happiest years of my life, so I knew the summer would be the icing on the cake. I was excited to get this course done, so that I could start the next chapter. Then something cataclysmic happened—I was about to fall in love at first sight.

The course was happening at Keele Street Public School. All the students were listening to this teacher from TVO, a publicly funded Ontario education television channel, who had us in stitches with his anecdotes. Twenty minutes into the class, the door opened and this vision walked in, obviously flustered because she was late, and sat down. She looked exactly like Farrah Fawcett, and I couldn't take my eyes off her. The way she was dressed, the way she took notes, the way she moved—way, way out of my league. But I was stricken; I had to find a way to get the courage to talk to her. Not exactly sure what else was discussed with the students, but my mind was scrambling for any idea to speak with her—without sounding like a dweeb. *Eureka!* In the period before lunch, I floated the idea to a few of my buddies in the room that we have a game of basketball at lunchtime in the school gym. There a was lot interested, so now I knew what I would do. I found out her name was Julie, and as she was walking down the hall for lunch, I called out to her and invited her to join the game. I figured since I was a basketball player, this would be a great segue into at least a conversation. She agreed. Being a basketball guy, as many in the class knew, I took charge of the situation and said I would be one of the captains. You obviously know what comes next. I had first pick, and I picked Julie. That was phase one. During the game, a guy from the other team was very rough and ran over Julie on purpose. Phase two came into action when I bodied him to the floor when he came into the key area. I was in like Flynn from then on. Not sure why true love isn't explained the way it felt to us—trains colliding, fireworks lighting up the entire sky, a vibrant, everlasting rainbow…We decided to get married a few years later on November thirteenth. It was the furthest thing from sunny—grey with a skiff of snow, but we didn't notice. It was one of the sunniest days in our lives.

When we had been blessed with a family, life was definitely unfolding the way we wanted. We faced the regular trials and tribulations every family experiences—mortgages, juggling schedules, and worrying about the turns in the road that children face. But all in all, we knew we could weather anything because we had each other and a strong belief that life would only get better.

As I drove with Jake to Toronto on that fateful November day, we did what we did best—laughed, talked about school, and competed with each other to guess the tunes and the musical groups on the radio. I have to say that I am pretty good at guessing song names and artists. The only problem with my skill is that I am only good from the years 1968 to 1973. Any years other than those is a struggle. I try to stay up with new music, but I'm afraid I have become just like my dad used to be back in the seventies. I would ask him to turn on 1050 Chum a.m. to listen to the new music of the day. He would last about a song and a half and then hastily reach for the radio to turn off that stuff. He spewed expletives as he changed the station to talk radio. I am that guy now when I drive around in the car. It's either oldies or talk radio. How did I get here?

Friday night in Toronto, driving to see the Toronto Raptors baseball team sets the stage for excitement—all the office buildings and stores lit up against the blackness of the night; buses and cars jockeying for position while people scurried along the sidewalk eager to get home or to be with friends at a neighbourhood pub or sporting event. Toronto was alive with activity, as the shadows of the city came alive. "Free Bird" was playing as I turned to check the traffic on my left before changing lanes. All of a sudden, I could feel a lump on the right side of my neck. Jake kept talking while I began to feel around my lymph node. *Come on*, I thought. *Take it easy. You're just getting a cold.* The rest of the night, I looked and sounded the same for Jake's sake, but my mind was racing. There was a creeping recognition of what this was, although, I didn't dare voice it. To speak the C word out loud to anyone at this point, I feared, would become a self-fulfilling prophecy.

Luckily, the basketball game was a good one. I lost myself in the game and watched as my younger son revelled in the game he loved.

When we got home, I showed Julie the lump, and she helped calm me. I'd had a cold; I could check it out with the doctor. Everything would be fine—just a blip on the radar. I was terrified; as we lay in bed, Julie comforted me and placed her hand on the right side of my neck—somehow, I drifted off, willing myself to stay positive.

Throughout the next few months, the lump didn't shrink away. A few weeks later at work, I joked with one of my associates that I should increase my life insurance. After I said that, a weird feeling came over me. I was kidding—but at the same time I wasn't.

One of the boys had to go for a physical. While there, I asked the doctor about the lump. He said we should keep an eye on it, but it probably wasn't anything, as I had had a cold not too long ago. Notice I didn't make an appointment for myself. I was too occupied with life and all it had to offer. I was on the treadmill and couldn't justify getting off to look after something as trivial as a lump on my neck. Work needed me, the family needed me, and I needed to be the man I envisioned being. The truth was I was playing ostrich—burying my head in the sand. I really thought that by not making an appointment took away the legitimacy of a problem. It would just go away.

November passed. Life continued with the busy pleasures—teaching, coaching, and supporting the development of two active boys. Julie and I loved the excitement and fulfillment of having a family, but with two demanding careers, we knew very well the sacrifices required for running the marathon of life. To add to the mayhem, I had become a fitness trainer, helping adults embrace activity and a balanced lifestyle. With a Bachelor of Science in Kinesiology, I put the degree to work in high school, teaching science and exercise science. Having an entrepreneurial spirit, I thought I

could do more with my education. I enrolled in the CESP course, Ca
dian Society of Exercise Physiology. The course ran every Tuesday night at
York University in Toronto from 6 to 10 p.m. It was just over an hour drive
each way. If I was going to train and shape people's lives, I wanted to have
as much training and education as possible. *Carpe diem*, seize the day, was
my motto as a trainer. With 1,440 minutes in a day, I encouraged my clients
to allow themselves thirty of these minutes for keeping fit. I became expert
at motivating others…but I still had this lump.

I can claim that the pace of work was what kept me from doing
anything about it, but the reality was fear. In my mind, if I didn't recognize
the possibilities of this lump, it would not exist. Yet, I was extremely body-
sensitive and always had been—I could feel the effects of a single Aspirin.
Really, I had a sickening feeling what the lump was, but I couldn't say it—I
wouldn't say it.

Christmas Day, 1999, saw the McCrone family breaking bread with my
brother-in-law, Roger, and his wife, Elise. Roger is not only family but also
a great friend. He is a gastroenterologist and probably one of the smartest
people I know. Trying to sound casual, I asked him about the lump on my
neck. After palpating my neck, he suggested I make an appointment to
have the lump biopsied just to be safe. I wanted to be reassured; I wanted
to be fine. But I knew.

I know what I have to do now.
I've got to keep breathing because tomorrow
the sun will rise.
Who knows what the tide could bring?
~Tom Hanks, Castaway

2

Make the World Go Away; Get It off my Shoulders

Have you ever had one of those mornings where you're not sure if you want to get out of bed and meet the day? January 20, 2000, was one of those mornings for me. This was D-Day—I was going to find out the results of the biopsy taken from my neck in mid-December. I had to wait through the holidays to get the results of the biopsy. It was a double-edged sword. There was enough going on throughout the holidays to keep my mind off the results of the biopsy. On the other hand, there was that fear of the unknown that was a constant in my mind. The uncertainty definitely took the edge off of the holidays. However, I always had a smile on my face. I had undergone a series of appointments with different doctors, all wonderful people who assured me that even with the full range of possibilities, from a cold's after-effects to cancer, the likelihood was that I would be fine. But, I was unable to shake the worry. I willed myself to be upbeat and casual for the sake of my family. However, when I was alone with my thoughts, the fear was, at times, all-consuming. When my rational thinking struggled for answers, it usually led me to a precipice overlooking a black abyss. How could I have cancer? I didn't smoke, ran every day, and was in great shape. I was the fitness guy! But, of course, cancer was indiscriminate about whom it chose. How would I handle it? How would I stay strong? How would I tell my wife? When would we tell the boys? How would the news affect them? Would I survive?

During the hour drive to the doctor's office, I was waging war with my thoughts. Positive versus negative—come on McCrone: "When the going gets tough, the tough get going." When I arrived at the doctor's office, I had my game face on and was determined to be positive. Surely, this would make a difference. Sitting in the waiting room, I saw nurses performing their daily routine; I thought this was just another doctor's appointment, and my life would continue as usual when I walked out of the office. I visualized sitting in front of the doctor and listening to him telling me the tests had come back negative and there was nothing to worry about. I would shake his hand and wish him a good day.

The ride home would be a good one; I had just made a new CD and was saving it for the ride. That was my treat to myself. Listen to the tunes cranked up loud and get back in time to see Jake play basketball.

It was a powerful mindset—I had used this visualization technique as an athlete when the competition was fierce. How many times had I been on the foul line in a basketball game with no time left on the clock and down by two points? I knew the power of focus, the determination of my will, and the belief in my capabilities.

The doctor entered the room with a file folder. I knew by the look on his face that the buzzer had sounded, and I had lost. He told me it wasn't good news. I had squamous cell cancer. The way I looked at it, even though in my mind the buzzer had sounded and I had lost, I turned it around to see the buzzer sounded, but the score was now tied. I now have an overtime period to win the game. My lymph gland was swollen because it had trapped the cancerous cells. So, the C word was out there—no escaping it now. I worried about everything at once: my life, my family's reaction, Auntie Ev and Uncle Ed's concern, and even how difficult this was for the doctor to convey the news. The first question I had and the only question that seemed to matter at that point was, "What was my chance of surviving?" Was I playing one-on-one with Shaquille O'Neal or a six-year-old?

Years earlier, I did come up against a formidable foe in a game of one-on-one basketball. I heard there was a one-on-one tournament held at a university thirty miles from the University I was attending in December before the Christmas break. Getting away to play basketball and take a break from studying seemed like a cool thing to do, even though I'd have to hitchhike to get there, having no car and no one who would take me. It was a Saturday, and it was snowing quite hard. I had asked a couple of friends if they wanted to go into the tournament, and they said no. So, I was on my own hitchhiking through a snowstorm. The tournament lasted most of the day and as the tournament progressed, I was charging up wins. Well, I knew with little rest between games would be a test to my fortitude and endurance, and I also knew I probably would be facing a seven-foot competitor. My goal was to make the final and play against this guy. I watched him play on my games off and came up with a strategy as to how to beat him before the final game. To sweeten the pot, the organizers told us the winner was going to get a gold watch, which was sponsored by a Canadian beer company. Boy, did that ever get the adrenaline running. This would be the best prize I'd ever won, so my game face was on. My strategy was to beat him to the basket, because if we are both under the basket I would not get a shot away. He was smart, as he laid off me and gave me open shots. The only way my strategy would work would be if my shots from the outside were going in. Then he would have to come out and guard me and being only six-foot five, I could drive by him to the basket. It was a very closely contested game, and I came out victorious by a very small margin. Close only counts in horseshoes, so this win was all mine! I was so excited to get that gold watch. It was as if I was a boy who got a pair of brand-new red shoes who walked all around town never taking his eyes off them. I must've checked the time a hundred times within that first hour. As I got back out into the snowstorm and stuck my thumb out to hitchhike back to my university, nothing could change the euphoric feeling I had. It was so fortunate that the university pubs were still open when I got back. It took me a while before I sat down at the bar. I had to go to every table and say, "Pardon me, do you know what time it is?"; "Oh wait, let me just check the time with my new gold watch." I still have that watch today.

I didn't care how I got the cancer; I wanted to know if I was going to live and for how long. The doctor emphasized the need to identify the primary site so that the tumour could be located, measured, and properly treated. There was no precipice now—I was in the abyss. Numbers would now dictate the course of my new reality: measurements, dosages, treatments, duration, and days.

Okay, so fight or flight was the option. I already had shifted into fight mode; the transition was immediate. I was in a crisis—no time to wallow in self-pity because this was the biggest game of my life. I needed to know what was next. How fast would things move along? Could I start treatment tomorrow, or at the latest the end of the week? We even considered going to the States for treatment at $100,000—by mortgaging the house it was doable. I willed myself to be prepared. Surely, the quicker I received the treatment, the better chance I had of surviving. The oncologist slowed me down and explained that the tumour had been growing for a while, and that numerous tests would have to be completed before any treatment was initiated. I hadn't thought of that. The cancer had been in my body for a while, and it was just now surfacing. When I think back to the fall of that year, I remember feeling tired quite a bit. I remember being in the fitness room and not having the usual spark or energy to get through a workout. What was once enjoyable and part of my daily routine had become very laborious. I remember catching power naps between classes. Why hadn't I figured out that there was something wrong with my body? The doctor assured me I wasn't going to die in the next month. I would be receiving a call in a few days about the scheduling of appointments. So, this was it. I got up and shook his hand and did wish him a good day. That part of my visualization did come to fruition—it was now up to me to make sure I would not let this new reality become my life.

I stood still outside of the doctor's office. It felt like I was in a movie where you see a character standing still and everyone else passing them is a blur. I did not want to be part of this scene. If I was to be part of a scene like this, I wanted to be one of the blurred images, just as I had been when I entered the building. The walk back to the car was surreal; everyone was still going about their daily routines, just as I had been one hour earlier. Didn't these people know I had cancer? Why didn't the world stop? I needed Julie; I needed her to make the world go away.

The drive home was silent. The CD never got played and never would be played. I was in shock; my worst fears confirmed. Pulling the car over to the shoulder of the road, I took out a scrap of paper and pen and wrote endless questions I hadn't thought of in the doctor's office. The silence was not only deafening but also sickening. I watched the cars rush by and felt strangely apart. For now, I just needed to plant one foot in front of the other. I needed to go thorough rituals of normalcy to ensure I would stay strong and positive. My family needed this from me—I needed this from me.

I had an hour to get my composure back before I walked into the gymnasium to watch my son play basketball. My wife was out of town helping with mass pool screening of candidates from York University and wouldn't be home until 10 p.m. A normal day with the usual routine was now becoming anything but normal. I just wanted to go home and have the family together, safe within the four walls of our home.

When I entered the gym, I had the feeling of looking down on the scene from far away. There I was sitting in the stands with a friend who had joined me to watch the game. His son was also on the team. As a spectator, I was going through the motions. Boy, was I good! My friend had no idea what I was going through. I should have been an actor. My son and I drove home. Since we were on our own, I suggested we stop for fast food. That was something we never did. He looked at me as if I was crazy. I said, "Let's go for it. Why not? You only go around once."

It's hard to say what preoccupied me more—defining my new life or desperately pining for my old one. I decided to call my brother-in-law, Roger, when I got home after Jake was in bed. I needed reassurance, and I needed a new vocabulary to help me understand the road I was on. Roger has a gift as a medical practioner—he is a teacher at heart. He had a way of teaching me about my new reality without patronizing me or trivializing the situation. I was trying to ready myself for one of the hardest things I had to do—tell Julie. Unfortunately, Jake had awoken and had come downstairs while I was on the phone. He passed me a note that said, "Dad, do you have cancer? Are you dying?" I quickly ended the call and held on to my son. I will never forget looking into his large, innocent eyes, which were pleading with me to make the pain go away. This was not the way I wanted Jake to find out, but I was going to get better, I told him. That was the only option. After some tears on both our parts, I sat with Jake as he drifted back to sleep, knowing my son's life had also changed.

So, now I watched for Julie's car to drive into our laneway. The way the lights reflected off the driveway and the way the trees looked with the light shining through their branches reminded me of a scene from a movie. Add thunder and lightning, and it would've turned into a horror movie. It was scary enough without the added sound effects. As she pulled in and turned the headlights off, I had a sense of foreboding. Julie is a very passionate person; she lives and loves deeply. Everything I had planned to say evaporated as she came in the door. While she was hanging up her coat, she was very animated, chatting enthusiastically about how much she had enjoyed speaking with young people. I pretended I was listening and making small talk. "That sounds good." "Really?" Julie accuses me of having selective hearing at times—well, this was off the charts in selective hearing. As she turned, Julie looked into my eyes and said, "What's wrong?" With no preamble, I let it escape, "I have cancer." There it was, the C word, hanging in the air like a poisonous gas. We cried, we talked, and Julie began to transition into her fight mode. She called family, friends, and my boss that night; to me, each call was like being lashed.

We didn't sleep that night; we held each other close, with Julie's hand on my neck where that persistent lump lay. We were both in shock, but we both knew we'd be locked together in the biggest fight of our lives. The next morning, we talked with Jake and comforted him with our love. Going to school for all of us would keep us moving forward. In particular, it would help Jake to be just a kid and escape from the weight of such a crisis. We agreed we would go down to Baltimore and tell our older son, Luke, face to face. He had won an academic scholarship to attend a boys' private school, Cardinal Gibbons, but it also was a great opportunity to play basketball at a higher level.

I should mention that I spent very little time in the *Why me?* phase. That wasn't going to help me in my fight. The *How did I get cancer?* phase lasted a little longer. During my quieter moments, I would try to figure out the cause. I had a cancer that mainly involved people who smoke or drank heavily. I was none of the above. There had to be a logical reason. Perhaps it was the smoky bars and restaurants I had spent so much time in. Maybe it was inhaling diesel fumes for twelve hours at a stretch while working on a drilling rig in Fort McMurray, Alberta, one summer. It was my third year of university; I had taken out a bank loan to finish the year. My funds had run out, and I was not eligible for any more student loans. To a nineteen-year-old, it was very scary. I remember someone a few years older than me at the time saying I would never be as rich as I was right now—never have the same amount of money solely for personal use. I looked at this person and thought he was crazy. If this was his idea of being rich, I wasn't interested. A few years later, I reflected on his comment and realized he was telling the truth—I now had a mortgage, car loans, food expenses for the family, educational and youth sport costs, entertainment expenses for the family, etc. Back in University I had just enough money for Marty. That was all I needed. I had money for food (not the healthiest by the way) and money for the pub. Life was simple, and yet I hadn't realized it. The summer between my third and fourth year of university had to be a big money maker, or I would not be able to continue my schooling. I had heard that a place called Fort McMurray, in northern Alberta, was paying three times the wage I was making back home. The operative word was "heard." No idea if this was true, but I was willing to roll the dice and find out. I had mentioned this to my roommate at the time, and we both decided we needed to head to Fort McMurray and make the big bucks. Without a car, we figured the only way to get out there was to hitchhike. Luckily, another friend from school just bought a new, used 411 Volkswagen, and he was heading out west to Calgary, Alberta. A 411 is not a big car by any stretch of the imagination. What should have been a thirty-six-hour drive, ended up considerably longer because we broke down twice on the way to Calgary. The drive from Calgary to Fort McMurray is eight hours. Hitch-hiking made it considerably longer. One ride took us to a small town called Athabasca. We met a guy from there who told us a story about wolverines, how they would make a sound like a baby crying to lure their prey out into the open. It was a good story—we had a great night that night. The next morning, we were on our way to Fort McMurray. Fast forward about a month, the two of us were sleeping in our small two-man tent when we heard what sounded like a baby crying. We remembered the tale the guy in Athabaska told us about how the wolverine would make a sound like a baby crying. We were scared out of our wits. We had a knife between us, and we moved closer together in the middle of the tent. We had no idea what we would do if the wolverine came into the tent. One thing for sure was we were not going out of our tent. Eventually, the sound went away, and we got back to sleep. It had snowed that night, and when we woke up in the morning, we could see catlike prints all around our tent. We said that morning that we were going to go out and buy a gun, which, of course, we didn't do and never again heard those cat cries outside our tent. When we got to Fort McMurray late one afternoon, we found a baseball diamond with an announcer's booth built on stilts about three stories above ground. We slept in the announcer's booth in our sleeping bags. It was right beside the Athabaska River, and you could hear the ice shifting throughout the night. The next day, we went into town and heard about a construction company hiring. We got a job that day. I had brought a small two-person pup tent with us. We found an area on the outskirts of town where people were pitching tents and trailers in a gravel pit. That was our new home for a couple months. The pay I received for working construction was great, but I needed more money. I got a job at the Alberta liquor store and worked there from five to ten most nights after my day job digging ditches. In June, my roommate went back to Barrie, and I stayed on in Fort McMurray.

In July, my brother came out to join me after I secured a job at the Athabasca tar sands working on a drilling rig. We worked from seven at night until seven in the morning, twelve hours a day, seven days a week. We would work through rain and snow. Swarms of mosquitoes arrived every day around four in the morning, and bugs called no-see-ems, could get in through the tent screening. Man, they were bad! We lived in trailers, and at the end of our shift, which was 7 a.m., we would head for breakfast after we showered and then head back to our single room where we would write letters or read a novel. There was absolutely nothing else to do. No computers, no Internet, no TV, just a radio. On the positive side, we saw the northern lights pretty well every night—that was our own personal light show. Our working mates were mostly Vietnam vets. We were a hard-working, no-nonsense, tough crew. This was definitely the hardest job I have ever had in my life. Just to set the stage, the tar sands were rich in oil. There were these huge machines that extracted the soil, which was rich in oil. Our crew would stay ahead of the extraction machinery and drill test holes to send down seismic equipment to make sure the soil wouldn't fall in onto the extraction machinery. It seemed we were always downwind to the diesel fumes coming off the drilling rig. Every night, I would feel squeamish breathing in those fumes. These fumes, I thought, might be the reason I contracted cancer, as there were many nights where I threw up from the smell. At the end of August, my brother and I had to leave as school was waiting. They cancelled our shift, so we could go into Fort McMurray to a pub with our crew. As I mentioned earlier, most of the guys were Vietnam vets, and we had not had a break for weeks on end. It was like a scene in a movie. We all sat together at a table playing drinking games. We got inebriated fairly quickly. One guy was carrying a lot of baggage from the war and drank until he fell asleep at the table. It was time to say goodbye to our coworkers because it was quite late, and we had all had more than enough to drink. That was a tough goodbye, as I knew I would never see them again. My brother and I spent the night in the back of my pickup, and we were off on the road early the next morning not feeling very well. I dropped my brother off in Calgary, and I continued on across the prairies in my '63 Ford Econoline pickup. I picked up hitchhikers along the way just as I had received rides on the way out. I broke down in Nipigon, Ontario, and spent two nights there waiting for a part. The fellow who owned the garage insisted I stay with him and his family. There is quite a community of Finnish people in Nipigon, and having a Finnish background on my mother's side, I seemed to blend in. It was a wonderful stay. A weird thing happened when I eventually got home. I tried sleeping in my bedroom, but I felt too claustrophobic. I think this was from living in a tent for months, and then working outside for twelve hours a night. I set up my tent in the backyard and slept there for a week before I went back to school.

Another thought I had about getting cancer was I used to play with mercury while in elementary school. You found a thermometer, broke it open, and played with the mercury on your desk with a ruler. If that happened today, the entire school would be shut down, and first responders with hazmat suits would be all over the school and the neighborhood. So what caused the cancer that was growing inside me? Perhaps, there was an even more plausible reason. We lived in an area in Oro where seven people had been diagnosed with squamous cell cancer of the throat—an astronomical number for a small area. One of biggest concerns was pesticide runoff from the farmland. Since we lived in Shanty Bay, we were lower than the farmland, which allowed the runoff to travel to Kempenfelt Bay. This was the probable cause.

I had other theories, but the bottom line was this: one cell out of trillions had decided not to follow the rules they were supposed to. Being devious, this cell convinced others not to follow the rules. Eventually, they formed a gang and waged battle with the cells that were doing what they were supposed to do—protect me. I wasn't going to let these deviant cells defeat the good ones. This was a true modern-day cellular *West Side Story*.

Being a competitive person, I approached this period in my life as a contest. One that I was going to win. Had to win. I needed a game plan, and

I knew that the doctors would provide me with one that would succeed. Waiting for the game plan required patience. I had this cancer growing inside me, and I wanted to start the game right away. A lot of attention has been given in the media to the healthcare system in Canada and its flaws. Stories of long wait times for treatment, people going to the United States for treatment. I was a little nervous. Would I die waiting to be seen? Would I have to travel out of the country to survive? My fears would be relieved as the phone calls from the doctors' offices started coming in within couple of days. The medical system was well organized. Everything moved along without a hitch. I was going to be so focused on getting through the treatment that nothing would stand in my way. I would do exactly as the "coach" said. It was the only way I knew how to handle what life had thrown at me. It was the only way to get it off from where it was, draped on my shoulder: "Make the world go away, Get it off of my shoulders..."

With these changes in latitudes,
changes in attitudes
Nothing remains quite the same
With all of my running and all
of my cunning
If I couldn't laugh I just would go insane
If we couldn't laugh we just
would go insane
If we weren't all crazy we would
go insane.

~Jimmy Buffett

3

Time Is on my Side, Yes It Is...

Our older son, Luke, was out of the loop when I went through all the initial medical appointments and testing. Luke was blissfully unaware in Baltimore. He was billeted with a family, and we had religiously gone to see him every month.

After getting the cancer diagnosis, we waited. We did not want to tell Luke until we had a plan and the prognosis. Julie and I decided we needed to meet with the radiologist and the ear, nose, and throat (ENT) doctor before speaking to Luke, so that we could give him the entire picture. Luke was fifteen and was on an academic scholarship at a private boys' school in Baltimore. How had he ended up in Baltimore? The previous summer we had sent Luke and Jake to Morgan Wooten's prestigious basketball camp at Frostburg College in Maryland.

Both boys had attracted a lot of attention and were offered opportunities at a few schools in the Baltimore and Washington areas. While this was all very flattering, we felt we had not had kids to give them away. However, our quiet, homebody son, Luke, told us he'd really like to try this thing. We were blown away! Jake had been recruited by Wooten's son in Washington, but he was only twelve, and we weren't about to have our sons separated. We thought that if this situation worked out for Luke, we would follow as a family, and Jake could also attend the same school as Luke.

I think back to the summer of '99 and how Julie and I would sit on the front porch night after night, working through the ramifications of Luke going off to Baltimore. We felt like we were Andy and Barney from

Mayberry, sitting on the front porch. Instead of whittling wood or peeling apples, we were trying to decide the direction our family was headed.

We had endless conversations, weighing the pros and cons while watching the sun set behind the trees. At the time, it seemed stressful. When I look back, it seems so serene. This was all we had to worry about—and it was a wonderful opportunity for our son. There weren't any health issues. It seems as we progress through life and are in present-day situations, which feel stressful, we look back at other situations that were challenging at the time, but now in hindsight they seem not as stressful as what we're dealing with in the present. It's all perspective and experience.

Life was unfolding as it should. Julie and I told Luke we would check out the school and its program and the potential home where Luke would be billeted. If everything met with our approval, we would let Luke make the final decision to go or not. In the meantime, Julie began to look for job opportunities in Baltimore, in and out of teaching; I would stay behind until Jake completed grade eight in Ontario. Julie would eventually land a job in a Baltimore suburb doing staff training for a company that built retirement communities. Her boss, Andy Aldi, was a creative genius—a boy wonder in the financial world. He had attended an Ivy league School, University of Pennsylvania, and spearheaded an innovative program to address the difficulty with getting employees for geriatric care. Julie was hired to help in this welfare-to-work project, where she would help young welfare women get their GEDs and then get their certification for geriatric nursing assistants.

Her work visa was to begin at the end of January, midway through Luke's first year in high school. Letting Luke go to Baltimore was one of the hardest decisions we ever made. While he was staying with a nice family and called home each night, our hearts ached to have him close. But Luke was happy and needed a challenge academically, which the school in Baltimore certainly provided. After I was diagnosed with cancer, we spoke with Luke's billeting family and let them know what was going on in my life. The father of this family was a doctor and reassured us that Luke could come to him with any questions after we had visited and told Luke the news.

The weeks after my diagnosis were a whirlwind. Julie called her new employer in Baltimore, who compassionately said they would hold her job for as long as she needed. I met with the ENT doctor, who told me I would have an operation called a quadroscopy, which would take biopsies from the base of my tongue and down my throat, to try to pinpoint the primary site of tumour. This was critically important in determining the focus of the radiation. The quadroscopy was the beginning of the journey. It seemed real now. I was going to a hospital, a place where I had not spent a single night in my life. We got there at 7 a.m. and did not get a room until 8 p.m. that night. Man, that was a long day, not to mention one doozy of a sore throat for days. Little did I know the sore throat was a minor league sore throat. The major league sore throat was just around the bend. After the quadroscopy, the ENT doctor said he did not have clear evidence of the primary site, but he did feel a slight roughness at the base of the tongue. It was at the midline at the base of the tongue. With this information, the radiation oncologist determined he would have to radiate both sides of the neck, which would ultimately mean the salivary glands on both sides of my mouth would be rendered useless. What? No saliva? Julie and I went home and read up on salivary glands during radiation. We felt relieved when we read that it *may* cause the loss of salivary glands.

The next morning, I met with a dentist specializing in cancer patients. She clarified that there was no *may* in my case, as both sides would get hit with radiation. I immediately asked to see Julie. When Julie came in, I know my eyes were shining with held back tears, pleading with her to save me. Julie said, "Oh, well. This is a small price to pay. That's the most important thing." She was right—game face, big guy.

A lack of saliva is a major dental problem. Teeth need saliva to stay clean and combat bacteria—saliva has natural enzymes that help protect teeth. If I had had this cancer twenty-five years earlier, the protocol would have been to remove all my teeth because they would have become rotten and fallen out for lack of saliva. I learned I would have to follow a careful regime (somewhat like people with braces) to maintain teeth and gums, including wearing upper and lower trays containing a decay-retarding fluoride treatment each night. But as Julie told me, this was a small price to pay for life.

Now, we had the picture. I had squamous cell cancer and needed twenty-five radiation treatments. The doctors believed it wasn't even a level one tumour, so my chances of a full recovery were great. We could now leave for Baltimore armed with good and bad news, but I was discovering something about myself. I couldn't tell people I had cancer, including my sons. Enter Julie. She was the opener so that I could be the closer. What a team! Just like Fred Astaire and Ginger Rogers. Who am I kidding? Most days we were like Ralph and Alice Kramden! In Baltimore, Julie, Jake, and I sat with Luke while Julie told Luke the news, quietly and sensitively. She outlined how the cancer would be treated and, most importantly, eradicated. I was then able to assure Luke that this was an unexpected turn in the road but that, with treatment and time, I would get back on track.

Obviously, we had to handle the information with Luke especially carefully. He was living a thousand kilometres away at the tender age of fifteen. We had to ensure he knew the diagnosis and prognosis at the same time, so that he would not be left in the dark so far from home. Jake and Luke had always been close and to be separated was difficult enough already. To be apart from each other in the face of adversity made this doubly hard.

There were a lot of tears on the way back home—worrying that what we had said was not enough. During the following week, Julie asked Luke if he had asked his host family any more questions about cancer. When Luke said he hadn't, she asked why. After a pause, he said, "Why would I ask any questions? You told me everything, right, Mom?"

Nothing is more valuable at times like this than faith in your family.

I can't change the direction of the wind, but I can adjust my sails to always reach my destination.

~Jimmy Dean

4

Middle Earth

When I woke up on January 20, 2000, I was defined as a husband, a parent, a friend, a professional, and an athlete. When I walked out of the doctor's office at three in the afternoon, my identity had been erased. I was now a guy who had cancer. Perhaps nothing puts you more into a niche than a small town. Barrie, Ontario, is now a city by definition of its exploding population, but it still has a distinctly small-town feel. Think of small-town living—and its drawbacks—as portrayed in Stephen Leacock's *Sunshine Sketches of A Little Town*, if you know the book. I had grown up in Barrie and had gained a little notoriety with basketball. Unfortunately, I was also acutely aware of the locals' pervasive desire to keep tabs on one another and neatly pigeonhole each resident for easy reference. Here is a quick example of pigeonholing each other in a small town. When I went to high school, there were only three in town. If there was a party, it usually consisted of students from all three high schools. For example, when I was in elementary school in the eighth grade, half of the students went to one high school and the other half went to another neighbouring high school. We all knew each other. A friend of mine decided that when we turned fifty, we should rent an old steamboat that would take us on a three-hour cruise. Luckily, Gilligan and the Skipper were not on board. I am so glad everyone had name tags because, after thirty years, a lot of us change. Julie and I were talking to a former classmate and her brother. The brother asked about our boys and where they went to school. I told him our eldest attended Harvard University. At that point, he leaned over to a sister and said, "Isn't Marty just a teacher?" There it was—pigeonholed once again in a small town. I knew only too well that whatever I had been pre-cancer would dissolve, as I would now become a cancer story. While I felt I would eventually be able to handle this, I knew it would be extremely difficult for Julie, who fiercely guards the privacy of family.

Treatment also meant I would be leaving the workplace. I loved my job, my students, my colleagues. There's that old adage: if you find a job you like, you'll never work a day in your life. That was me; the everyday inter-actions had been priceless, as I realized all the more as I was leaving every-body in my social world behind. Now, it was my family and me hunkering down to withstand the cancer adversary—team McCrone vs. team C. Let me rewrite that previous couple of words: team McCrone versus team c. I just could not write the word cancer with a capital c. It does not deserve the recognition a capital letter warrants.

My new social network was reduced to complete strangers in waiting rooms. Our family calendar was replaced with appointment after appoint-ment. Social entries were wiped clean. Life was on hold for the whole fam-ily. When someone gets cancer, the entire family gets it. It felt like we, as a family, had entered a subculture of the sick. We had left the surface of the Earth where all the healthy people lived and played and were now living in Middle Earth. I'm not talking about the elf and hobbit inhabited realm you might know from J.R.R. Tolkien's writings. The Middle Earth I mean isn't an enchanted place in any way, shape, or form. It's an in-between land, one that hovers between real life and the shadows of the Underworld and the darkness of death. While other people carried on with their lives, I had become invisible. I felt alone, scared in this unknown territory. Through-out my life, I had always been athletic, loving the whole exhilaration of movement and competition. I had never smoked and was only a social drinker, yet still, I had descended here—how devastating! Perhaps worse than anything was dragging the whole family into Middle Earth. I could see the heartbreak and fear in their eyes; I could hear the anger in their voices. Why? Anger was not a feeling I was willing to indulge—I had to show them I could handle this and that they did not need to rail at our shared misfortune. Everything would be fine, wouldn't it?

Middle Earth is a lonely place to be. Apart from the medical appoint-ments, life consisted of endless phone calls that my wife would return during the evening. E-mail was not a tool most people used at this time.

The phone calls were important for us as a family. They were a link to the land of the healthy and living. They were a direct line to the surface.

Life on the surface of the Earth is, in a sense, like a giant video game. If you are born with a hundred percent health, you are lucky. A lot of people start off in the game of life with compromised health. Just like *Mario Brothers*, you continue through the game of life trying to build up as much health as possible. This health is not only physical health but spiritual health, mental health, occupational health, financial health, etc. The object of the game is to get to the end of our life with as much health as possible, while avoiding various antagonists that try to diminish our strength and our health. Things like disease, car accidents, mental illness, mishaps, and physical injuries are constant threats, and we have to do whatever is required to survive. At times, we diminish our own health through unhealthy eating, addiction, etc. When cancer is the issue, the threat from the disease itself is compounded by the danger of allowing our mind and ego to buck at reality, especially during the initial stages. To us mere mortals, disciplined as we are to seek order in things and make sense of them, the fear of the unknown is overwhelming. We find ourselves in Middle Earth. Something similar can happen as a result of a divorce, the loss of a career, retirement, or any number of other crises that strip us of our identity. To move forward, it is essential to discover new meaning and new goals. Facing loss, we have to remake ourselves, forge a genuine new self. Out of adversity comes renewal and resurfacing into the Land of the Living. The disease no longer defines who we are; instead, it goads us to find our authentic self.

Waiting for someone to say,
"Hello in there, hello."

~John Prine

5

Identity Crisis

When I was living in Middle Earth, cancer defined me. It was like the sheet that had been draped over me, had become me. I was the shroud of cancer; it was who I was now. No more teacher, coach, father, husband. After the initial shock, I knew there was no choice but to fight this formidable foe; but as I battled through the operations and treatments, I realized that who I thought I was had been replaced with what I had contracted. I was the new cancer boy; I was the new hot topic at the local Starbucks. "That's Marty McCrone. He used to be a great basketball player. He's got cancer, you know." I became invisible to some, a discomforting reminder to others that anyone can be hit with a debilitating illness. The process of losing your identity or your perception of who you are is quite subtle at first; but I began to realize ever more keenly that people were not responding to me the way I had become accustomed to. As my physical being changed and I lost weight and gained a sickly pallor, my illness became obvious to others. I was not receiving the smiles, the "Hi, how are you?" that I used to get. A few people remained the same, but most of my interactions with strangers and some friends had become furtive glances and a conscious turn away.

I had left the society I had known for forty-five years. I was now invisible. Part of one's identity is answering to everyone else's needs and expectations. I had gone from a job where I had hundreds of human contacts on a daily basis to barely any. I had lost my sense of worth or belonging. My position at work was filled within a day. How could that be? All the systems I had in place to make my classes run smoothly were for naught, replaced by someone else's structure. How would anyone be able to take over and do the same job I had done for the past fifteen years? Wasn't I indispensable? Someone explained the "bucket of water" theory to me a few years later. Saxon Kessinger's poem explains it well:

There Is No Indispensable Man
by Saxon N. White Kessinger

Sometime when you're feeling important;
Sometime when your ego's in bloom;
Sometime when you take it for granted
You're the best qualified in the room,

Sometime when you feel that your going
Would leave an unfillable hole,
Just follow these simple instructions
And see how they humble your soul;

Take a bucket and fill it with water,
Put your hand in it up to the wrist,
Pull it out and the hole that's remaining
Is a measure of how you will be missed.

You can splash all you wish when you enter,
You may stir up the water galore,
But stop and you'll find that in no time
It looks quite the same as before.

The moral of this quaint example
Is do just the best that you can,
Be proud of yourself but remember,
There's no indispensable man.

The hole that my absence had created at school disappeared almost instantly.

I wasn't recognized now for anything but having cancer. So this is what it would be like in Middle Earth. I was afraid.

There is a group of people who live in the central highlands of Africa. When they meet each other on the trails, one person says, "Good morning, hello. How are you?" The answer is not "I'm fine; how are you?" The answer translated into English is "I see you." Think about it. I see you—I acknowledge you, I value you, I respect you. We all have a basic need to be seen for who we are; we need to be recognized for what we contribute. Entry to Middle Earth can be through many doors—illness, retirement, loss of job, loss of marriage, empty nest. Middle Earth shrouds each member in a blanket of forgetfulness—not between its inhabitants, but on the part of most people in the land of the living.

It was the recognition of what was happening that inspired and motivated me to get through the crisis.

Susan Sontag wrote of time as a powerful force blowing us through the tight tunnel of the present into the future. When it came to my struggle, I pictured two lakes separated by a narrows. The first lake was who I had been until this major change in my life. That lake defined me. It represented how I saw society and how society saw me. The way I had developed my core values and beliefs was the underpinning of my character. I was proud of who I was. I lived in a society that acknowledged and respected my positive role. My most coveted accomplishments were being a husband to the love of my life and being a father to my two cherished boys. And I tried to sustain all this and my professional identify even after the cancer experience was upon me, and I had moved to Baltimore. In Baltimore, I was offered a teaching/coaching job at a private Catholic girl's school. Daily positive interactions with students and colleagues reinforced my pride, my sense of self-worth. I still remember the day I was interviewed for the job. Julie accompanied me to the school and waited outside the office where I was being interviewed. Keep in mind, I was still down sixty pounds and not looking that great. In the interview, the principal, head nun, Sister Mary David, asked me if that was my wife in the hallway. I answered, "Yes." She went out on into the hallway and asked Julie to join us for the interview. The reason for the sister asking Julie to join us had nothing to do with my state of health; Sister Mary David wanted Julie a part of the process as the coaching and teaching commitment needed to be embraced by the family, and the family would also become a part of the Mount de Sales community. I'd never experienced an interview like this, which was both intense and welcoming. The athletic director, Paul Randazzo, was putting me through my paces, not so much about my knowledge of athletics, but in how I would be able to handle the intense pressure of the community. At first, I was taken aback that perhaps my answers weren't addressing what Paul was asking. Interestingly, it was his passion and his incredible intelligence that immediately made me think we'd make a great team.

I was to wear several hats at the school. I would teach science and physical education, be the assistant athletic director, and coach varsity basketball and varsity volleyball. So here I was, a Canadian. teaching in a city that was a hotbed for varsity athletics. How would I be perceived? Would parents and other coaches think of me as less qualified coming from Canada? Paul Randazzo helped me understand that the majority of the parents would be more than supportive—only a few would be irrational about the capabilities of their daughters. He made it clear that he'd help me navigate those waters. I think Paul appreciated my style right from the get-go when I told my players that I wasn't a yeller. I would instruct and correct in practice. Games were for putting into reality what they had learned. I also told them it's just like parenting: manners are taught in the home, not out in public. Paul never forgot that and loved repeating that story. For me to be with someone for a mere three years out of my life, and for that relationship to become one of the closest friendships I've ever had, would be astonishing. The belief that we should keep ourselves open to new possibilities never resonated more than that friendship—and it remains as strong and meaningful today.

My first week teaching in the classroom was so strange to me. The students were doing exactly as I asked, and you could hear a pin drop. This was so foreign to me. I thought, *I cannot do this for much longer.* I had to insert my personality into the classroom. I think they thought I was a little crazy in the beginning. I could feel myself slowly coming out of Middle Earth. I was the varsity basketball coach and the athletic director, and I was also offered the job of varsity volleyball coach. I said sure. I had coached and played a little volleyball back in Canada, but I wasn't up-to-date with all the new systems etc. Our boys both played volleyball at a high-level, so

I recruited them to help me out with some practices. With the boys' help and me purchasing a really good book of drills, I was ready to become a volleyball coach in the USA. The first year, we were in the B division, and we went undefeated and won that division. Wow, this was fun! The second year, we were moved up to A division, where there are a lot of club players and powerhouse schools. When you move up from one division to higher division, the expectations aren't that high. As it turned out, we started winning games. When you win games, everything is great. Parents are happy, players are happy, and Marty is happy. In the final playoff tournament at the end of the season, we went up against the first-place team in the gold medal match. The practice the day before the championship game, I said to the players, "It feels like Christmas Eve when you are so excited it's hard to get to sleep."

The next day, the parents were all wearing Santa Claus hats to the games! That's the kind of great, supportive parents I had. We ended up losing in the championship game, but what a successful season. I received a phone call about three weeks later from the sports editor of the *Baltimore Sun*. She said that I was chosen as Baltimore City, Baltimore County, Coach of the Year in Volleyball. I told her I didn't know there was such a thing and asked her if this was a good thing? I asked her why was I chosen for the Coach of the Year, and she said she had been watching me for two years and liked the way I was with the players. She was impressed that, even though we didn't have any club players, we made it to the finals of the A division. This was unprecedented. Once again, Marty was happy. Before I could redefine who I was, I had to travel through the narrows to my new identity. This period of time in the narrows will differ with individuals—I was there for three years. I had spent so much time nurturing others—family, students, coworkers, friends—that I had not centred on my needs. My goals had been clear, but I could not see myself yet; more importantly, no one outside of my family and close friends saw me at all. Getting healthy was my new goal, but regaining an identity in the land of the living was dependent on my journey through the narrows and into a different lake. Cancer had changed me, but it wasn't who I was.

My new social network consisted of strangers I met in waiting rooms. It was fascinating to talk and observe these fellow inhabitants of Middle Earth. They, too, were struggling to regain their sense of self. We had all suffered a loss of identity and were in different stages of grieving. The narrows is not a straight paddle—I would often go back and forth between stages, lingering at a sense of loss in the mist. I knew, however, I had to keep moving forward. I kept remembering the time I was paddling a canoe across a large lake into an extremely strong headwind. I was by myself in the canoe and every time I took a break from paddling, as I was starting to fatigue, I would lose ground against the formidable headwind. After an hour and a half paddle, I made it to the other side totally fatigued. I was not going to be defeated. For some reason, I portaged the "Why me?" region. Once I realized that I had trillions of cells that had not mutated, I simply wondered, "Why not me?"

It was refreshing to see individuals who were near the end of their treatment, or those who were coming back for follow-up appointments. Those lucky ones had left Middle Earth and were putting their toes into a new lake. The journey out of Middle Earth back to the land of the living happens on three fronts: physically, mentally, and spiritually. Unfortunately, it's not a simple case of making your way out of Middle Earth on all three fronts at the same time. There were days when I fell back from the land of the living on a spiritual basis but was still in Middle Earth physically and mentally. A good day could be defined as being out of Middle Earth physically, mentally, and spiritually, all three. Those were fabulous days! Getting back physically took a long time. Being very active all my life, I missed being able to exercise—that was an excruciating loss. It seemed like eons before I could start working out. The first time I went back to the gym, I couldn't even lift an empty barbell. I had to get one of my sons to spot me. Gone was the guy who would pause in front of a mirror to check out his pipes. One aspect of exercising that I most missed was getting the heart rate up and breaking a sweat. It was a couple of years before this happened. Part of my daily routine now is to exercise every day. When I feel lazy, I think back to the time when all I wished for was to be able to break a sweat. This is just another one of those cases where you don't know how good you have it until something is taken away from you.

The journey out of Middle Earth is personal and self-directed. While support groups were available where I was, I believed that having the family together in Baltimore would speed up my recovery. Still, moving to Baltimore cut me off from the life and friends I had known. Julie was off to work; the boys were at school. And me? I was stuck in the narrows bottoming out with my despair. I was depressed for at least three years. I worried about expressing my fears to Julie. Expressing myself has never been my strong suit, and depression further compounded my reticence. Before I got the job at Mount de Sales, I would spend the day watching the Biography Channel and a show called *Whatever happened to...* I was relegated to being a voyeur—I was on the sidelines of the game of life. I had lost myself. I wondered whatever happened to Marty McCrone. In retrospect, I should have pursued the counselling Julie had encouraged me to get. There was a huge amount of irrational guilt for putting my family through such heartache. When Julie and I talked, I tried not to burden her further with my spiritual struggles. When she pleaded with me to get counselling, I balked. When I regained some of my stamina, I realized two things that were invaluable: I had cancer, and I would be a different person because of it. I was beginning to see that "new lake" and future possibilities. I wanted people to say, "I see you. Hello." On the one-year anniversary of my diagnosis, January 20, 2001, the boys, Julie, and I went out for a really nice dinner at one of them-there-fancy-restaurants. That's me channelling my inner Earl voice! (It'll make sense in a later chapter.) The boys could order anything, even stuff on the right side of the menu. Once we ordered the food, Julie and the boys handed me a small gift-wrapped box. I started to wonder if I had missed an important occasion. Should I have a gift to give to someone? I proceeded to open the box, and inside the box was a soft cloth bag. I still had no idea what I was opening. Inside the bag was a gorgeous gold ring. They explained to me it was a story ring. It has six sides to it and each side was engraved to represent parts of my identity. The six panels consisted of a basketball player, a picture of two wedding rings, a picture of a golfer, a picture of a guardian angel, a picture of two boys, and a picture of stacked school books. Wearing the ring help me realize who I was. I was not cancer; I was everything on that ring.

This taught me that "I see you" is about living in the moment. It is about life now—this second. It is about allowing the past to drift away. It is about stopping the mind's incessant need to plan the future. Life is what it is—it is the moment: I SEE YOU!

Oh, yesterday's over my shoulder
So I can't look back for too long
There's just too much to see waiting in
front of me
And I know that I just can't go wrong.
~Jimmy Buffett

6

Unbelievable Timing

The day after I was diagnosed with the first cancer, I went to work. I worked with two really close friends, and I had to find a way to tell them. I called them into my office and said that I had had a bad day yesterday. Before they could ask me what had happened, I explained that I had been diagnosed with cancer. The P.E. office was a meeting place for faculty and students alike to come and hang out. We had an old couch along with our desks and filing cabinets in the office. It was the nucleus of the school. Students would come down with their problems or when they weren't feeling well, and they could sleep on the couch. It was just a nice safe-haven for everyone. We had so much fun in that office. There was a student named Mary who was in my Phys Ed class. Every day, she would come to class early to borrow my moisturizing cream. The cream was always on my desk. "McCrone, can I borrow your cream?" And every day, I would say, "Sure, Mary. Go ahead." She would pump little spots down each arm and down each leg, put the cream down and then spread it. One day, I decided to empty the cream into another container and fill the cream container with LePage's white glue. *Knock, knock, knock!* "Come in! Hey, Mary!"

"McCrone, can I borrow your cream?"

"Sure, Mary. It's right there on my desk." I kept my head down at the desk and gave a few little glances as I saw her spot her legs and arms with the glue. When she had finished putting on the cream a.k.a. glue, she started to spread the glue. I got out of my chair and decided to walk quickly out of the Phys Ed office. She came running out after me, and I was bent over crying—I was laughing so hard. Another quick story, you entered our

Phys Ed office through one of two hallways that entered into changerooms and our office. Therefore, we had two entrances into our office. One time, I decided to get professional looking signs made to put on our doors to our office. The signs read, "Please use other door." We had a custodian affix them to the doors to make them look authentic. Without a lie, the first person we tricked with the signs was the principal of the school. We could hear her high heels click as she walked to the doors. She read the sign, went out of the hallway into the gym and back into the other hallway to the other door. Here she read, "Please use other door" again. Then we heard a delightful laugh. I believe those signs are still up to this day. There are so many other stories that I could tell with regards to the environment we had at that school. My two cohorts and I shared so much—a love of life, family, sports, and teaching.

Now after I'd uttered the c word, the three of us just sat and stared blankly, unable to find words to convey our feelings. The c word for many is a death knell—I really had no idea of what the future held or where the path I was on would lead. I did know that everything was about to change and some part of me was detaching from this workplace, from these friends, to an experience none of us had had. This was not something they could help me with—I had to fight it on my own. I knew this was my battle.

The three of us were in a state of shock. One of the friends later said that when I told him I had had a bad day, he thought I was going to say that I'd been in a car accident. Never did he expect to hear the c word. We carried on throughout the day, trying to find things to laugh and talk about, anything other than cancer.

After lunch, the three of us were standing in the middle of the gym, as we all taught Physical Education. We had a triple gymnasium filled with over a hundred students. We always gave them plenty of time to shoot around and just have unstructured fun. I was drinking a can of Diet Coke, and my two friends kept talking to me, trying to help me focus on the day. A girl in my ninth grade P.E. class came up to me and said, "You shouldn't drink that, sir." I said, "Why?" and she replied, "It could give you cancer." I told her, "It's too late!" We all broke up, laughing so hard, tears came to our eyes. The girl walked away, looking puzzled, wondering what exactly the joke was. It was a good thing that she did not understand the situation.

I think of that scenario a lot, of how ironic the timing was. No one had ever said, "It could give you cancer" to me in all my years of teaching. I guess it was one of those inexplicable situations. In the moment, believing that things happen for a reason can be comforting. For instance, if Julie and I had succeeded in landing jobs in Baltimore in the fall of '99 and had moved the family there then, I probably wouldn't have acted on the lump in my neck. Being in a different country with a vastly different healthcare system, I would have avoided going to the doctor. By the time the symptoms had become worse and I felt compelled to seek help from an unfamiliar medical establishment, the cancer might have spread throughout the body. At the time, we were disheartened that we couldn't make the move to the States to be with our son, Luke. Since then, there have been other disappointments along the way, sometimes with a favorable result in the end. Such ironic coincidences are just that—coincidences—but they give us the humility of realizing that sometimes we're just plain lucky, not out of any special merit. In the end, believing that all things happen for a reason does not sit right with me, as I've known so many people who lost their battle with cancer and were just unlucky. Period.

Allied with that perspective is the sense of humour that has always been important to me. My family and best friends seek out the amusing side of any situation, so there was little surprise that in facing the adversity of this illness, humour would be a large part of my arsenal.

In my next visit to Princess Margaret Hospital, a leading cancer research and treatment facility in Toronto, we met with the radiologist who would be assessing the number and intensity of the radiation treatments I would receive. Being an athlete at six foot five and 220 pounds, the doctor calculated he should up the dosage and reduce the number of treatments from the usual thirty to twenty-five. Julie thought this was a bad idea because my body was so sensitive to what it took in—I could strongly feel the effects of one Aspirin, for example. Ultimately, I chose the twenty-five treatments, which would prove to be a lot to handle. Quietly, Julie told the doctor that she only wished she could be the one undergoing the treatments instead of me. The doctor reassured her with platitudes, basically telling her that hers was a normal reaction from the caregiver. Deadpan, Julie said, "Oh, no, I just meant men make the worst patients, and I'm not looking forward to dealing with the whining!" Julie and I both broke up, laughing until our sides hurt as the shocked doctor left the room, shaking his head. Come on, a little dark humour wouldn't kill us if this other thing didn't.

Love when you can,
cry when you have to,
be who you must,
that's all part of the plan.
~Dan Fogelberg

7

Sweating the Small Stuff

Being in the cancer game means many appointments and tests in order to determine how the doctors will proceed with the treatment. Sometimes, I would hurry up just to wait. I learned to block out the whole day when I had an appointment. That way if the appointment was on time, or the tests went smoothly, I got out in a timely manner, and I felt wonderful! It's all about self-talk. I chose to think positively and visualize success. This was a mantra for me. Ever since I began sports, my coaches would emphasize: "It's not if we win, but *when* we win." Of course, these tests I had to undergo were all new to me. I hadn't even had an X-ray in my life other than at the dentist's office. Julie accompanied me to all the appointments. I had heard of the tests, but I had no idea what they entailed. The X-rays were a piece of cake. The CT scan was more involved, as the technicians injected dye into my blood stream and then scanned my body. Each test took a day, factoring in the two-hour commute to the hospital, the waiting, the testing, and the commute back. The MRI test was a challenge. If you have an MRI done on another part of your body, it isn't as confining as the MRI done on the head and neck. MRI stands for Magnetic Resonating Image. I was placed on a table and secured to the table so that my head and neck could not move. Earplugs were inserted to muffle the sound of the magnets when they started to resonate. They were quite loud when the machine got going. The table moved me into a long encasing tube, the top of which was a few centimetres from my face. I had to go to a different place in my mind to keep from feeling claustrophobic. The technicians talked to me to reassure me throughout the procedure. I imagined myself on a tropical island, basking in the sun. I was there for approximately fifty minutes—an eternity where, in order for the image to be accurate, I could not move and could only swallow periodically. This was tough. If I swallowed, I would have to stay longer in the tube to allow them to get an accurate reading from the scan. I remember swallowing during one scan. I was mentally ready to leave the tube because they had told me I would be finished in a couple of minutes. All of a sudden, the technician told me I had swallowed during one of the reads and they had to do another scan. I became very claustrophobic, and it took all the willpower I had to get back to the tropical island before I began to freak out. Luckily, I held my composure, and the final scan was successful. Another time, I remember sitting beside a fellow in the waiting room just before an MRI. He seemed very loose, almost dopey. I asked him what was going on. He told me he had to take a few sedatives to get through the confinement of the MRI. He went before me and within minutes came back through the waiting room. He was unable to handle it; despite being medicated, he became extremely anxious, and claustrophobia had set in. He couldn't stand the confinement of the tube. He had a lump in his neck just as I did. He would have to travel to the United States to have the MRI completed. Apparently, in the United States, MRI machines are available that aren't as confining. I felt sorry for the fellow but understood his plight.

A very close friend of ours, Joan, had the best line about waiting for an appointment. In a waiting room, she heard other people complaining about how long they were stuck there. She said to them, "I'm just glad I'm here every week, and I can wait." She was glad to be there as opposed to... the other option. Her patience and kindness were virtues we all aspire to have. I have used that line so many times in waiting rooms.

One of my most memorable appointments was at the beginning of my journey through Middle Earth. Julie and I were in the basement of Princess Margaret Hospital. The appointment was to have a plastic mask made for me to wear when receiving radiation. This mask attached to my head and neck would then be bolted to the table. This would prevent movement and ensure the accuracy of the beams of radiation. When they told me I was going to have radiation to the head and neck, I had no idea what that entailed. I had a vision of sticking my head into a machine shaped like a big square box. That was how ignorant I was about the cancer world and what treatment really meant. I remembered a few years earlier when we were vacationing in Florida. We would walk by a local medical centre and see the word "oncology" on their sign. I hate to admit this, but I didn't really understand what exactly that medical specialty was. Why did I need to know what it meant? It had no relevance to my life or the lives of my family. When I talk with people and use some cancer terms, I understand their naivety. I hope they never have to learn the language of cancer.

So here we were in the basement of one of the premier cancer institutes in the world. The basement of any building to me isn't an inviting place—below ground level, often without much light. When I think of it, the beginning of my journey to Middle Earth started with me below the surface of the Earth in this hospital basement. Narrow white hallways where people in white shrouds would move from room to room. There was always an eerie silence hovering in these subterranean hallways as we would make our way to the "mask" room. It felt like we were in a movie, and we were in the basement of an insane asylum. Not what I had envisioned. First a mask needed to be created in plaster, and later a plastic mould would be made of my face.

It was terrifying and claustrophobic to have plastic wrap put over my face with holes for the nose and a straw in my mouth. Then plaster was applied and had to set for about fifteen minutes. I was expecting Dr. Frankenstein to come into the room. The reality of radiation was looming.

But something happened…a life-altering moment occurred to which both of us so often go back and remember with reverence and hope. As we sat clutching each other's hands, a young man in his mid-twenties accompanied by his mother was seated across from us. He had a black eye-patch on, and while he was obviously a handsome young man, one side of his face had been reconstructed. There was an artistic symmetry about him as he sat with his legs swung over the next chair, his long black hair rakishly brushed back from his face—we couldn't help but look at this young man. His mother returned our gaze protectively. She told her son she had to go back out to put money in the metre for the car. When she left the room, the young man looked at us and shyly said, "You'll have to excuse my mother. She is always on the defensive when I am out in public." We struck up a conversation, and he explained how he had undergone surgery and radiation to remove cancer from his cheek. Unfortunately, the cancer had returned just as he had been preparing to return to work. This time, a tumour had been discovered at the base of his brain, and he had lost vision in his left eye. He looked so longingly over at us when he said, "It has been so long that I've had to worry about the big things in life. I was really looking forward to going back to work and just being able to sweat the small stuff again."

There have been so many times when we have thought of this wonderful young man and his gift to us in that moment. We have offered countless prayers for him as no one else has ever so poignantly expressed to us the simple pleasures of living and appreciating now. Each time we visit Princess Margaret Hospital, we hope to run into him to thank him for his wisdom. Sadly, we never have, but we dearly hope he is sweating the small stuff again and loving it.

If life seems jolly rotten,
there's something you've forgotten.
~Monty Python

8

Radiation Time

Before my first radiation appointment, a day was set aside for a mock run-through of the procedure. My mask was placed on my head and bolted to the table. The radiation oncologist proceeded to make a number of marks and figures on my mask as he lined me up for future real treatments. My mask looked like a calculus teacher had written the lesson plan all over the it—or, I was the son of Frankenstein! This was serious stuff. Two small tattoos (dots) were inscribed on my chest to provide points of reference for the technicians to line my body up with the radiation beam. These tattoos would be permanent souvenirs to remind me of my experience.

How hard could twenty-five treatments of radiation be? The radiation technicians were fabulous. Over the five weeks, we became very close. They explained to me that everyone reacted differently to the radiation and that some people could carry on a relatively normal life during the treatment. I was hoping to be the poster boy for radiation and treat it like a walk in the park.

Like the mask room, the radiation treatment rooms are in the basement of Princess Margaret Hospital. You go down a few floors and swipe your card. This lets the technicians know you have arrived. I had asked for mid-morning appointments, as I had an hour-and-a-half to a two-hour drive each way; the PMH staff were more than accommodating. You had to be very patient when you arrived. Some days the machines went down, and there would be a one- or two-hour delay. Other days, the technicians would encounter patients with further problems, and there would be delays. Once inside the treatment room, the treatment only took fifteen to twenty minutes. There was a beautiful picture, a seascape, as you entered the room. During the session, I could bring in my own CD of the tunes I wanted or listen to the ones they provided.

I lay down on a steel table with my mask on my head. The mask was, as advertised, bolted to the table to eliminate any movement. Once aligned, the technicians left the room, and I could hear a brief buzzing. The foot-thick lead door opened, and the technicians came back into the room to realign the radiation beam. When they left, I could hear the buzzing again. It only lasted a few seconds. This procedure was repeated four times. After the last beam, I was unbolted and free to leave. Man, that seemed easy, only twenty-four sessions to go. I said my goodbyes and drove an hour and a half home. At this point, I could drive myself. The effects of radiation are cumulative, therefore, you don't feel the first few rounds of radiation. A piece of cake! The corollary to that is once you're finished radiation, you deal with the side effects of radiation for a long period of time, even though your radiation has come to an end. I knew it was going to get worse, but I held out hope that I would be the one who didn't react adversely to the radiation. The technicians talked about an elderly gentleman who went to work every day through his radiation treatment. I wanted to be that guy. As it turned out, I was the poster boy for the opposite reason: I was known for showing how brutal radiation can be. To this day, when I go back for checkups, the doctor brings in students and shows them the extreme side effects of radiation treatment. Actually, they have asked me to be part of a study examining the effects of radiation. I feel it is my duty to give back to the hospital in any way that I can. The study will entail me undergoing more MRI's. Yikes!

The radiation therapy lasted for five weeks. Man, they were tough weeks. The hour-and-a-half drive down, and the hour-and-a-half drive back seemed okay in the beginning. But as the days turned into weeks, I got weaker and the pain just kept getting stronger.

After radiation, I had to have more tests completed to see if the radiation had eradicated the cancer. The only viable option was to have an operation called radical neck surgery. At the beginning of this whole process, we knew this operation might be a possibility. It is a major operation where they basically remove muscles, nerves, and vessels from your neck. The major side effects of the operation would be the removal of one side of my neck, a loss of mobility to my neck and arm, and an accumulation of lymph fluid under my chin.

The five-hour operation was performed on May 15, 2000. When I was coherent a few days after the operation, I looked at myself in the mirror. Yep. That's Frankenstein with half a neck! There were numerous stitches and staples in my neck. People visiting me put on a good act because it was not a pretty sight. After a week in the hospital, it was back home where home care personnel came in every day for a month to tend to the neck.

The summer of 2000 was spent trying to put on weight and wean myself off my painkillers. I had an analgesic patch on my arm that emitted morphine throughout the day. Through the summer, the home care nurse slowly decreased the strength of the patch until I was on Tylenol 3s. I then went to Tylenol 2s and eventually by the end of August; I was pain- and drug-free.

My life seems divided into two parts. It's like life before and after you have children. Things change dramatically. I refer to life before cancer as my other life. Physically, emotionally, and spiritually, things are different. That's a story for another time. As mentioned earlier, the side effects of head and neck cancer are severe. I have a dry mouth every minute of every day. This will not change over time. I moisten my mouth with water and beverages every couple of minutes. I have tried every artificial saliva product on the market, and they are all short-term solutions. In the beginning, I took a sip of water every couple of minutes when I was trying to sleep. The doctors said I would get used to sleeping with a dry mouth; they were right. After about a year, I was able to sleep or should I say lie in bed without having to drink water every couple of minutes. Six years out of treatment, I will sip five or six times a night. Of course drinking water all day and throughout the night causes you to go to the bathroom more than normal. I am up a lot throughout the night using the washroom. I view sleep as just a bunch of small power naps throughout the night.

Throughout the day, I have a bottle of water with me at all times. I need to sip every minute or so. If I get caught without my water, it is very uncomfortable, especially if I run into someone and start talking. Yikes!

I can't remember what it is like to eat a meal and not have to put a liquid in my mouth to lubricate the food enough to swallow. Saliva helps break down food during chewing, and without it, I need a liquid just to get the food down. If I go to a restaurant and I don't bring my water with me, I am held captive until my drink arrives. If there are munchies to eat on the table, I have to wait for my drink. All this becomes tiresome at times, but for the most part, this is my normal, and I do it without thinking about it.

Is this the real life?
Is this just fantasy?
Caught in a landslide
No escape from reality.
~Freddie Mercury, Queen

9

Blood Lab

If you are having trouble grasping the concept of Middle Earth, you just have to sit in the waiting room of a blood lab in any major cancer hospital.

Sitting in the waiting room chairs are frightened, desperate inhabitants of Middle Earth. Picture a cave under the ground with hollow-faced, weak, beaten down creatures with different looks in their eyes—some of hope, some of despair, and some of final surrender.

I would give a sample of blood only to have to wait a week or two to see how I was responding to treatment. Prior to becoming ill, my life was punctuated by celebrations and milestones—graduation, marriage, career, birth of our children—the normal stuff of life. Now my future in the blood lab was determined simply by a number. This number, which held no significance in my life before I became ill, now held the key to my future. I became well versed in the lingo of Middle Earth.

There is very little conversation in the waiting room of the blood lab. The majority of the people in the waiting room simply sit and watch or listen for their number to be called. Very few read magazines or newspapers. However, I found that striking up conversation was infectious. Everyone I spoke with was only too happy to share his or her experience, fears, and hopes.

When their number was called, they quietly got up out of their seat and headed into one of the many stations to give blood. Their identity was double checked with the record on file at the hospital. Very little small talk was exchanged between the lab technician and the patient. The technicians are very good at reading people. They respect what the patient is going through and will make light conversation if they sense in the person that they be open to talking. Speed and efficiency were of the utmost importance. A silent prayer by the patient would probably accompany the taking of blood—anything to help and perhaps to influence the results of the test.

The Middle Earth inhabitant knows the routine: wait a week or two and then see the doctor to find out the result of the blood test. Throughout the wait, self-doubt and self-analysis prevail. Will the blood test be a favourable reading? If so, how will I celebrate? How will I deal with bad news? Can I handle undergoing more treatment? How and when will I tell the family?

People in Middle Earth speak a different language. It is a language of medical terms, numbers, and dates. It is an exclusive club—even a caring spouse cannot gain admittance. I now make a habit to visit each department at Princess Margaret where I had treatments and appointments. I feel a need to give back after all I have received. When I see people at the beginning of their cancer journey, I sit down and talk with them. It's important to see someone who understands, who has lived in Middle Earth and returned to the Land of the Living.

A friend of mine suggested that I should speak to people about my experience. My first talk was to approximately 200 people. The days leading up to the presentation were spent sitting on the back porch outlining and planning my speech. I was practicing my speech but also rehearsing keeping my emotions in check. I found when I was finished giving my presentation, people came up to me and opened up, telling their own story. There was, in one of my talks, a person in the audience who I knew. He came up and said he really enjoyed listening to what I had to say. Fast forward a few years, and I met him on the street. He informed me that he was battling cancer and he made reference to the talk he had being in an attendance a few years ago.

He said he really didn't understand the Middle Earth analogy until he was diagnosed with cancer. He said, "I get it, I get it now." From then on, I have given many talks. The presentation is an excellent tool to get people talking and to help them help others who may be in Middle Earth. One of the things I encourage in people to do is to get out of their comfort zone and take the time to talk with others who may be going through a rough period. A week after one of my talks, I received a phone call from someone who had been in the audience. She said she was a teacher who had noticed at one of her basketball practices a girl of about ten years of age who looked like she had been dealing with some cancer issues. She said the child appeared to have lost weight and her hair looked like it was coming back after chemotherapy. This teacher said she was so moved by my speech she went up to the girl and her mother and struck up a conversation. It turns out the little girl had been going through some cancer treatment. The little girl really loved basketball but hadn't been able to play it for some time because of her sickness. Since I also run a basketball camp, this teacher wondered if we might be able to do something for this little girl. Between the teacher, the mother of the child, and me, we were able to arrange a free week of basketball camp for the upcoming summer. The mom let me know her daughter was thrilled to have something to look forward to—like she used to feel. She was making her way out of Middle Earth. The ten-year-old girl and I talked to the entire camp (180 campers) about our experiences. She related how when she would ride the bus to school, other students would mock her and say mean things to her because she had lost all her hair and didn't look healthy. What a teachable moment this was to the staff and campers.

I received the ultimate lesson—that life wasn't about me but about my service to others. The terms I used to define myself previously were no longer of importance. My life now was how to serve others. How could I become a service leader? How could my experience help? This was my way of giving back.

You can't always get what you want
but if you try sometime you will find
you get what you need.
~The Rolling Stones

10

Walkin' the Dog

Four out of five weeks of radiation treatment had been completed. Travelling to Princess Margaret Hospital in Toronto was an hour-and-a-half to a two-hour trip each way. Julie had taken time off to accompany me to all the pre-radiation appointments, so she arranged a series of drivers to take me to the treatments. The list of friends willing to take a day off and drive to Toronto was humbling. One of my friends who had multiple luxury cars allowed me to choose which car I could ride in. I still remember one trip to Toronto with him, I was having trouble keeping things down. We had to pull over in an apartment building parking lot, so I could throw up. Every time I go by that parking lot, which is a lot of times throughout the years, I remember that particular drive. There were so many memorable drives down with fabulous friends who took a day out of their schedule to drive me to Princess Margaret Hospital. Another option I had was to stay at the Lodge in Toronto. This is a place where, for a nominal fee, I could stay Monday to Friday and receive a shuttle bus to and from my appointments. Julie and I thought it was best for the family if I went down to the hospital each day. At least that way, there would be some normalcy to our life and to Jake, our younger son's life. It was important for me to see my wife and son every day and to be seen. With my older son away at school in the States during this time, Jake needed support from both his mother and father.

I feel very fortunate to have family and friends. I was blessed by growing up in the then small town of Barrie, Ontario. Watching *Leave it to Beaver* as a kid, I wished life were as simple as the one portrayed on the TV show. Little did I realize that we did, indeed, live in a simpler time. As a young boy in Barrie, I would leave my house, riding my bicycle with my friends early in the morning and return home before the street lights came on. The entire day was devoted to play. No adult interference, no family calendar filled with lessons and games, just simple play. Throughout those days of elementary and high school, I had a group of friends who have remained friends and, for the most part, still reside in the home town. The passing years have shown that we have a special thing going on. People have commented on how lucky we are to still have the bonds linking us when we were young. A line from the movie *Stand by Me* has always stuck with me: "Never had any friends later on like the ones I had when I was twelve—Jesus, does anyone?" My friends and I are very fortunate to have each other after all these years. I hope I am not portraying a "Glory Days" scenario, where the best day of our lives were behind us. We have all succeeded in our own endeavors and all respect each other's occupations and paths in life. In the summer of 2006, six of us went on a week-long trip to Huntington Beach, California. The week coincided with a surfing championship. We checked into a '50s-style motel right on the Pacific Coast Highway directly across from the beach—Surf City, USA. We could have easily stayed in a five-star hotel but elected to return to a simpler time. We had the greatest week. We bought a $19.99 barbecue, assembled it, and had cookouts in the parking lot of the motel every night, watching the sun set below the palm trees and the ocean. The motel was filled up with surfers who were there for the surfing competition. In the evenings, we would fire up the barbecue, turn up the tunes, which were obviously oldies, have a few beers, and hang out. A funny thing happened. All the cool surfer dudes and girls started to hang out with us. Comments could be heard such as, "I wish my parents were as cool as you guys." Those nights were like a scene out of a movie. We were kids again. The nice thing about our relationships with each other is that we are who we have always been. Harry Chapin said it very well: "Old friends mean more 'cause they can see where you are, and they know where you have been."

On the drive down to Princess Margaret for treatment, the regular drill was listening to the oldies in the background as we conversed. Near the end of the five weeks of radiation, I really didn't bring a lot to the conversational table as I was very sick and weak. I remember one rainy Monday afternoon in March when I returned home. I had lost sixty pounds; I had been using a numbing mouthwash before I would ingest my morphine orally. It was the only way to tolerate the liquid morphine because of the burning inside of the mouth, a burning that was preventing me from I taking food or water orally.

I couldn't tolerate the pain any longer. I phoned Julie and said I needed to go to the hospital. That night, we ended up at Credit Valley Hospital. I was admitted to a quad room. Later that night, one of the roommates passed away in the early morning hours. The family of the expired patient was there in different states of grieving and crying. I had never been in a situation like that before. Again, I could hear the cameras rolling as yet another movie scene was playing out in front of my eyes. I was in panic mode.

The next day, I was admitted to a private room and spent the next five weeks on morphine and IV. I couldn't put anything in my mouth, including water. I should have had a feeding tube inserted in me a few weeks prior. This would have made sure I was getting nutrition and proper hydration. I was stubborn and a little fearful of having the tube inserted, so I let on to everyone that I was doing just fine. It was a desperate effort to cling to normalcy. When I was being weighed on a weekly basis, I would stuff my pants with change, my cell phone, anything else I could find to help weigh me down. How stupid was that? I was so manic about not letting on how badly I was feeling. Truth is, I didn't want to admit it to myself, but Julie knew and had tried to get me to go to the hospital before this.

The stay in the hospital was just what I needed. I received my nutrition and morphine intravenously. The nurses and doctors were fabulous. A number of people visited me. Sometimes the morphine took over, and I imagined people in the room. I watched two episodes of *Law and Order* a day along with *Magnum PI*. Fortunately, I don't remember the episodes, so I can watch them today and still think I am seeing them for the first time! Actually, I think I watched the same episode twice each day.

When I was lying in the hospital room and looking out the window on a grey, rainy April afternoon, I saw a man out walking his dog. He had no patience, waiting in the rain for his dog to do his business. You could see that he was yammering and yelling at the dog. He was pulling him hard to different spots so that the dog would find the desired place to dump his load. Here I was lying in the hospital room, not having eaten or drunk anything in weeks, badly burned inside and out, drugged up on morphine, and looking feeble after losing the sixty pounds. All I thought of was how lucky the man was and how I would trade places with him in a flash. To this day, it doesn't matter what the skies are like outside, you will never hear me complain about the weather. If it is unbearably hot out, I say it is tropical. During the running of our basketball camp, Thunderhoops, we will get a few hot and humid days. I framed it to all the campers that the word hot is not a name. At our basketball camp, we use the word "tropical" instead of "hot." On those tropical days, I would have these eight- and nine-year-olds coming up to me and saying, "Marty, it sure is tropical in here." I would break up every time they said that. And in writing this, I'm laughing as I type. Still cracks me up! That just conjures up a better picture in the mind—tropical evokes vacation time. I also walk my dogs through any kind of weather, enjoying the moments and feeling glad I am able to be out with the dogs.

Focusing on the simple pleasures is what I choose. It is a realization of the moment and an understanding that this moment is all we ever have. There is no yesterday or tomorrow except in our minds—they are mirages. Appreciating the moment provides the joy and peace. I remember my radiologist saying that through the cancer ordeal, I would come away with a true appreciation of life. At the time, I was incredulous as I told him, "I didn't need cancer to appreciate life—I already do." In retrospect, there was some truth to what the radiologist said. I am determined each day to notice—really notice—the beauty around me. My wife has called me Pollyanna at times for my insistence that every day is a beautiful day. Julie and I were travelling in the car on a grey, cloudy day and I mentioned to her how beautiful it was that day. I commented on the different shades of grey in the sky and across the landscape and how the grey road we were travelling bisected the hues of grey. Well, Julie really thought I had lost it that day, but no. I am determined to relish my existence and also make a difference to others and really 'see' them in all their beauty.

After a workout at a local health club, I break the silence in the locker room and start up conversations with people. Sometimes, I feel like Norm from *Cheers* when I walk into the club now. It's my way of giving back the kindness I've had from others. I mean, it couldn't hurt, right?

Listen as your day unfolds.
Challenge what the future holds.

~Des'ree

11

Lobby of Major Cancer Hospital

I vividly remember the first time I entered the lobby of Princess Margaret Hospital. On the left, there was a quaint coffee shop; the smell of
the freshly brewed coffee was comforting. Around the lobby, people were
selling homemade crafts, someone was playing a piano, and lots of people
were sitting in chairs relaxing, at least so I thought. My first impression of
the hospital was that it was a very warm place to be. Surely this can't be
the dreaded cancer hospital! I was expecting something more morose and
sombre. I was thinking perhaps that this cancer thing I have wouldn't be as
bad as I thought it would be.

Not knowing where to go, I stepped up to the information desk. The
desk was manned by volunteers; they were ever so friendly and helpful.
They eased a lot of the anxiety my wife and I were feeling. Many of these volunteers have their own stories to tell and volunteer to give back to society.

Being a beginner is a recurring thing in life. I was a beginner when I
first learned to walk and talk. I was a beginner when I went to school for
the first time. I was a beginner when I got my first job, my first car, when I
started out in marriage, then in fatherhood. I was now a beginner in being
sick. I would imagine the people sitting in the lobby could spot a first-timer
in the lobby quite easily. A first-timer looks lost, scared, and full of trepida-
tion for unknown things to come.

After having entered the lobby at least a hundred times up to now,
I am no longer a beginner. The coffee shop I once cherished now has a
new connotation. When I enter the lobby and smell the fresh brewed
coffee, it brings me back to those dark days of radiation treatment. My

blood pressure increases and my heart races as I pass the coffee shop. I find myself taking a deep breath. Even when I am out in public and smell brewed coffee, it brings me back into Middle Earth. It has to be a form of PTSD. Both physiologically and mentally, it upsets my homeostatic state. It's like I am reliving those terrible days that were so hard to get through. But it also reminds me of Joan, Julie's Matron of Honour and one of our dearest friends. We were comrades in battle, hers against the formidable foe of breast cancer and mine with squamous cell cancer. We would agree to meet at the coffee shop—it was our place, our refuge.

I now understand why the people in the lobby are sitting so quietly. Some are waiting for a shuttle bus to take them back to an off-site residence where out of town people can stay Monday to Friday. Instead of driving back and forth from their hometown, they can stay at the residence as they receive treatment. These people are in various stages of their treatment. They sometimes spend quite a long period of time waiting for the shuttle; no one seems impatient. They have learned that they are fortunate to be able to wait.

Actually, having talked to a number of the people waiting, I can say that they enjoy sitting and watching the people go by. It's their small journey out of Middle Earth and back to the surface. Another group of people sitting in the lobby are the volunteer drivers. These wonderful people donate their time driving out-of-town patients to the hospital and back. Those who don't want to stay at the residence have an option to be driven from their hometown to the hospital. These volunteers will drive to the hospital in the morning and wait for hours for their passengers to receive treatment. Through heavy traffic and adverse weather conditions, they carry their precious cargo. Conversations in the vans are usually upbeat. Deep friendships are made during these travels. There is a connectedness; most of these drivers also have their stories. Giving back unselfishly, these drivers understand how important it is to see the person and not the cancer. They are of service.

I didn't see the significance of having entertainment in the lobby until I became a veteran of the hospital and lobby. Some form of entertainment happens on a regular basis. It could be someone singing, playing the piano, or a small group of musicians performing. The musicians donate their time to the hospital. Just recently, I stayed to take it all in. I had no idea how powerful this musical interlude was to the dynamics of the hospital and, more importantly, the lobby of the hospital. People came from their hospital rooms to take part in the hour-long presentation of music. I stood back and observed. It felt like these people came out of their caves from Middle Earth, remembering and being reconnected to life by their memories.

The audience consisted of people living with cancer—either the caregiver or the patient. Most of them had made the journey from their hospital room to the lobby. Intravenous apparatus accompanied some of the observers. The audience reminded me of warriors in battle who for one hour had a reprieve from the fighting. This was their stepping out of the present reality into the memory of other times and places—sweet reverie. They were totally lost in the music. I tried to fight back tears but wasn't successful. I will never forget the scene in the lobby that day.

When I go back for follow-up appointments, I spend time sitting in the lobby observing and talking to the warriors and volunteers. Being a seasoned veteran of the lobby, I can usually spot first-timers there. It's their eyes that give them away. I hope they take the time to understand the dynamics of the lobby. It truly is transformational—situations change, alter the persona forever—but never erase the power of the music, of who we are.

Walk like a man, talk like a man
Walk like a man, my son
~Frankie Valli

12

Birthdays

Life is punctuated by the significance we place on a moment, an event, a birthday. Birthdays vary in importance as we travel life's highway. The double-digit birthday is a significant one to a nine-year-old. Becoming a teenager, hitting the age of majority, turning thirty, all mean different things to different people. Julie and I, as parents, always put a positive, fun emphasis when a significant birthday was on the horizon. When Luke turned ten, we went on a road trip to Ann Arbour, Michigan, then continued on to Chicago. In Ann Arbour, we walked around the University of Michigan campus and went into the football stadium to have a look. That blew me away. The boys were overwhelmed. Needless to say, we went to the Ann Arbour bookstore and bought so much University of Michigan paraphernalia that it lasted for at least ten years. After Ann Arbour, we were on our way to Chicago. A friend of ours played for the Orlando Magic, and he got us tickets to see Orlando play Chicago in the old stadium. The boys were going to be able to see their idol, Michael Jordan, play live right in front of them. Before we went to the game, we went to a famous restaurant in downtown Chicago called Ed Debevic's. It was a theme restaurant where all the servers were seemingly rude to the customers. We didn't let the boys know this, and it was so much fun watching them react to the overbearing, rude servers. We let them know it was all a joke, so they could enjoy the rest of their meal. Near the end of dinner, I realized we were in a different time zone. This just meant we really had to hurry to get to the car and drive to the stadium, which was on the south side of Chicago. As an aside, every time I hear "Southside of Chicago," it reminds me of the Jim Croche song "Bad, Bad Leroy Brown." So here we were before Google maps, so you can appreciate the panic with Julie reading the map, riding shotgun, and me trying to navigate to the south side of Chicago. It all worked out. We found parking quite a distance from the stadium, went to the will call, got our tickets, and were seated for the tip off between the Orlando Magic and Michael Jordan with the Chicago Bulls. The year was 1994 when Michael was in his prime. After the game, we hung around to see our friend, but unbeknownst to us, they immediately got on the bus. When we came out of the stadium, there was nobody around. It was a scary situation because we were not in a very good neighborhood. A cab pulled up and asked us what we were doing. You could see the concern on his face as this might not have a good ending. I explained to him what had happened, and he said, "Get in my cab. I'll drive you to your car. Once you're in your car, follow me until I wave at you. Then you will be safe." We dodged that one!

When Luke became a teenager, we thought it would be cool to go to the Rock & Roll Hall of Fame. The boys were both well-versed in the old days and could name artists and songs of most songs from the '60s and '70s. The Rock & Roll Hall of Fame seemed to be a logical choice for somebody turning thirteen. We drove to Cleveland and stayed in a really nice hotel close to the Rock & Roll Hall of Fame. We also took the boys to Cleveland Science Center, which blew our minds. It was such a hands-on experience. The Rock & Roll Hall of Fame was an overload of memorabilia from the rock and roll era. The Beatles, the Rolling Stones, James Brown, Aretha Franklin. The list goes on and on and on. It is a must-see exhibit. On Jake's tenth birthday, we hired a limousine to pick up the boys and their two friends. In the limousine, the boys drank pop and smoked chocolate cigars. They were dressed to the nines, and they went to an expensive restaurant. Julie and I followed them in our car and sat a few tables from them in the restaurant. Boy, did they feel important!

For me, turning forty wasn't a big deal. I thought there was too much emphasis placed on the number forty. Me, I have always felt forty-five would be the coolest birthday. I like the concept that celebrating my birthday for just one day is an injustice—celebrations should last at least a week! My wife has taught me a few things...

March 24, 2000, was the day I turned forty-five. I had looked forward to this day for the past year just as I did as a nine-year-old in anticipation of those double digits. The day also fell on a weekend—that is always a bonus! Having a birthday on a Monday is just not right; neither, when you're young, is having a birthday in July or August and not being celebrated in school. When diagnosed in January, I still felt I would be able to celebrate in style. However, my optimism in holding out for a memorable birthday was fading along with my strength as I approached the date.

I had completed four weeks of radiation therapy on my neck with one week remaining. I was in rough shape. I had lost sixty pounds at this point. My mouth was so badly burned from the radiation that I couldn't put any food or water in my mouth. The liquid morphine was too painful to ingest.

On March 22, I had made the trip to the hospital to receive radiation and then back home by late morning. As usual, I had a close friend drive me to and from the hospital. It wasn't the road trip I had envisioned on my birthday. I think I only threw up once on the trip. A good day!

Home alone, I thought about where I was and where I had come from forty-five years ago. Julie was at work, and Jake was at school. Luke, our older son, was in Baltimore, Maryland, attending high school. This would be the first time the family wouldn't be together on a birthday. If there was a time I needed the entire family all together, this was it.

Jake was thirteen and attending a school thirty minutes from home. Before I got sick, Jake and I would travel to school together. Unfortunately, I wasn't able to drive him to school during this period. In times of adversity, family and friends contributed greatly to help keep some semblance of normalcy within the family while sacrificing their own routine. A close friend with whom I worked and with whom I ran Thunderhoops, Paul Hopper, offered to drive Jake to and from school most days. This added approximately forty-five minutes to an hour to his day. This was not a problem to him as he is a true team player. Now, there were some days where he was unable to drive Jake either to school or from school due to meetings or his coaching schedule. On those days, a neighbour of ours, who is also on staff at Twin Lakes Secondary School in Orillia, would drive Jake. You couldn't get two diametrically opposite personalities if you tried. My teaching partner, who drove an old car that he inherited from his dad, always played Bruce Springsteen. Conversation was upbeat, and they talked a lot about sports and music. On the other hand, our neighbour drove a nice Saab and played classical music. I once asked Jake who he would like to ride with the next morning. I said, "Jake both people are available to drive you to school tomorrow, who would you like to drive with?" You don't have to be a rocket scientist to have figured out with whom a thirteen-year-old would drive to school. He said he would rather go with my co-worker so he could listen to Springsteen, but most of all, he liked the smell of gas in the car. There must have been a gas leak somewhere in the old car. Oh great! We're sending our kid to school every day in a car that could blow up at any minute. At least, they weren't smoking cigars or cigarettes on the way.

When Jake arrived home from school, he would have a snack and would sit and watch *Walker Texas Ranger* every day with me—that was our routine. It wasn't a great show, but we were together and poked fun at Walker and his co-stars. We would get lost in the show and forget all that troubled us. Jake and I still talk of those special times together; they were truly precious moments. Even now we often remind each other of different episodes.

When I would get home from the hospital road trip, I would go upstairs and sleep in the afternoon. I would get up in time to greet Jake at the door when he returned from school.

On March 22, I was upstairs napping when I thought I heard Julie's voice calling me; I thought I must have been dreaming. Julie wasn't due home from work until a few hours later. I heard her gentle voice again calling me to come downstairs. This was not part of my routine, so I was a little dazed.

I slowly got out of bed and made my way downstairs. Negotiating stairs was not an easy task at this stage in treatment, so Julie met me halfway down to assist me. She reassured me that there was something special in the living room. I turned and saw Luke standing in the middle of the room. Tears flowed and wouldn't stop. I backed out of the room not wanting my son to see me this way. Julie comforted me and put everything in perspective with, "Jake sees you every day. Let Luke be a part of your life—he can handle it." Luke told me I looked great and walked toward me with a smile. His hug brought on a deluge of tears as I gave into his acceptance and love.

Luke's school in Baltimore had collected enough funds to fly Luke home for a surprise visit to celebrate my birthday. Julie had taken the afternoon off work and had driven to the airport to pick him up. That was the ultimate birthday party; I couldn't have scripted a better surprise!

I could only imagine the thoughts and emotions racing through his head as he saw me for the first time since my treatments had begun. We told him back in February that everything was going to be okay. How could he believe that, seeing the condition I was in?

Jake arrived home from school shortly after. The family, all together again, sat and watched *Walker Texas Ranger*. Jake and I couldn't upset our routine and miss an episode of the "Man."

What a party weekend! It wasn't what I had envisioned over the past year, but far better. We celebrated all weekend with family and friends dropping in. Julie, however, was not convinced that I was handling it. Despite her reservations, I was on a high being with everyone. The fact that I was unable to keep anything down—including water—was reaching a critical point.

On the Monday following the weekend, I was admitted to the hospital for six weeks. I hung onto those birthday memories during the hospital stay.

Live right now,
just be yourself.
It doesn't matter if it's good enough
to someone else?
~Jimmy Eat World

13

What Gotcha?

It was the spring, and I was out riding my bicycle when I needed to stop at a gas station to fill up one of my tires. This was in downtown Orlando. Julie and Jake were living in downtown Orlando, as Julie was teaching at a prestigious private school, and Jake was attending the school. Luke was off at University, and I was back home in Barrie, teaching. I had taken a three-year leave of absence to recover and to also teach in Baltimore. At the end of the three years, I had to make a decision. Resign from the school board or come back to teach in Canada. Obviously, I came back to teach. So just a quick recap of our crazy life. The boys went to a basketball camp; there they were recruited to come to Baltimore to play basketball and go to a private school. As a family, we were to go to Baltimore altogether as Julie and I had secured jobs. Marty ruins that plan by getting sick. Eventually, we all make it to Baltimore. We finished up in Baltimore, but Jake still had two more years of high school. Julie and Jake go to Florida, and I go back home. Meanwhile Luke is in *that* University. Some people look at us and think we are crazy! After I wrote this, I reread it and agree with those people. We were crazy! Talk about a long commute. I would make it down to Florida once a month and also come down during the longer holidays.

Back to the garage and filling my bicycle tires in Orlando. The mechanics and a few friends were standing around having a cigarette, and one of the guys asked me, "What gotcha?" So much weight and poignancy were carried in that simple statement. Flashes of the last year streaked through my mind. Having endured radiation in my neck for squamous cell cancer, I had been brought decidedly to my knees, and at six foot five and 220 lbs, that took a lot of force. I lost sixty pounds, ending up in the hospital for six weeks and having to relearn how to eat and swallow without the luxury of saliva. Just as I was beginning to recover, the doctors concluded I would need a radical neck dissection. I had a degree in science so the term "dissection" was familiar—but even if you're not a frog—never a good sign!

My ENT doctor operated and removed one side of my neck along with some muscles in the shoulder. As a result, my neck is somewhat normal on the one side but really doesn't exist on the other. The peculiar shape is quite noticeable, and I find people staring at me all the time. In the beginning, I would always wear a turtleneck in the wintertime and a collared shirt in the summertime when I was out in public. Then it occurred to me that I was hiding part of my new identity, and I shouldn't feel ashamed of how I looked. From that moment on in the summertime, it was T-shirts, baby!

So this everyday guy at the gas station was acknowledging me; he was saying, "I see you." I told him I had had cancer, and the bunch of us spent the remainder of their break chatting. I really admire people like the garage guy. He was a straight shooter and didn't try to sneak a glance when I wasn't looking. I have come to realize that people with physical deformities, whether minor or major, are constantly subjected to stares. I wish people would just come up and ask me what happened. In asking, people are recognizing another human being who perhaps got a bad break. I, in turn, am doing that when I see someone with a visible difference and speak to them about it. The experience reinforces that the truth really does set you free.

In most cases, people enjoying sharing their story. They are not embarrassed or too sensitive to explain. Talking, not avoiding the situation, helped me heal, and get farther out of Middle Earth. It's better than having this elephant in my living room that nobody wants to bring up.

I recently met a person who had a conspicuous scar across his face. We looked at each other and simultaneously asked each other what happened. We had an excellent conversation, and I felt like we were two warriors who had met after battle and were pleased just to be there, able to talk about what was ahead.

I haven't run into one person who didn't want to talk about what had happened to them in life; as the folk singer John Prine sang in his song "Hello in There"; inquiring into someone's situation is acknowledging the importance of their life. Everyone is important and precious. I needed to be acknowledged and to be recognized as part of the Land of the Living.

So if you are walking down
the street sometime
And spot some hollow ancient eyes
Please don't just pass 'em by and stare
As if you didn't care, say,
"Hello in there hello in there"
~John Prine

14

Hello in There

I was back at Starbucks (I think I'm hooked) having a frappuccino and reading the paper. I drink frappuccinos because they are cooling on the throat. Not having saliva, I find the drink soothing. I can make a frappuccino last close to an hour and a half. I know frapuccinos are not the best for you, but I can rationalize anything. "You poor boy, Marty. You have no saliva; therefore, have a frappuccino and feel better." I have a hard time remembering what it was like to have saliva. I remember when I first started feeling it diminish. It was the Friday at the end of the first week of radiation. The way radiation therapy worked for me was that I would go for treatment Monday through Friday and then have the weekend off. Julie rode shotgun, as I drove the first week as it takes a while for the debilitating effects of the radiation to build up. On the Friday, I stopped for a coffee and a muffin after treatment. I was pretty proud of myself. One week down and I felt okay. Perhaps this whole cancer gig wasn't going to be as bad as they had said. I left the coffee shop with my frappuccino and the muffin. I had an extra lift in my step. A little bit up the road I took a bite out of the muffin. Something wasn't right. Was this muffin stale? Why didn't it go down my throat the way it should? I kept chewing, and the consistency of the muffin didn't really change. It was nearly impossible to swallow the muffin in my mouth. I had to accompany the muffin with a sip of coffee to get it down my throat. My optimistic mood walking into the coffee shop had been replaced with fear and the realization that this was going to be a long, hard battle. All that weekend, I cherished what saliva I had left in my mouth. As the radiation progressed throughout the weeks, my saliva disappeared. The radiation beam had eradicated all salivary glands on both sides of my mouth. Now it is just a way of life: I have a drink with me at all times. Most of the time, it is a water bottle. There have been occasions when bottled water isn't allowed into certain venues. I try to sneak my water in without anyone seeing me. At times, they have found the water bottle and have tried taking it away from me. I don't like using the medical card, but sometimes you have to say. When I explain my situation to them, they usually let me take the water in with me. There have only been a few times where I ask to talk with the person in charge if they won't let me in to the venue. It's a very uncomfortable situation, especially for someone who is used to following the rules and appreciates why there are certain rules. Eating was difficult to get used to; with every bite of food, I have to drink some liquid to get the bolus of food down the esophagus. This was extremely uncomfortable at the beginning, but like everything else, I got used to the new reality.

While sitting on a nice soft couch in Starbucks, I noticed a gentleman around forty years of age. He sat down at a table near where I was sitting. He appeared to be with his mother. The gentleman was wearing a baseball cap, and his clothes fit him rather loosely. I had seen that look before—it was obvious he was undergoing some form of cancer treatment. He averted his eyes from others, and his mother seemed to be trying to comfort him.

I had a choice to make: walk away or go over and talk with him. I was an outgoing person before I got sick, but was only at ease as long as someone else initiated the conversation. I always admired people who could strike up conversations with total strangers; I was never one of those people. Since being ill, I have turned into one of those people. I don't go overboard and become annoying—at least I don't think I do! Striking up a conversation with a stranger is a cinch. A lot of times, we don't because we have judged that person on appearances alone and have dreamed up some rationale not to approach them. I was not going to judge a book by its covers, an old cliché, but one that conveys truth. I have opened and read so many of these "books" lately. It enriches every day of my life. I have met no end of interesting people along my journey. Just recently, I was at a local coffee shop. The fellow standing beside me in an adjacent line was in his sixties; half of his face had skin grafts on it. Again, I could have gone ahead with my day, purchasing my coffee and leaving. I thought this looked like an interesting book and one that wasn't opened very much because of its cover. I commented on the weather and then mentioned that it looked like he had gone through a tough time. I asked if it was cancer. We had an excellent conversation standing in line and carried it on after we received our coffee. I could see other people listening in. As it turned out, he had had cancer fourteen years prior and was thrilled that he had beaten the cancer. Here stood two warriors from Middle Earth sharing a few moments on the surface of the happy and healthy.

Back to the guy on the couch with his Mom. I stood up and went over to the table and offered them my seat on the couch. They replied they were okay sitting at the table. I then asked him if he was going through some cancer stuff. He said he was and offered me a seat at the table with his mom.

It turned out he had the same type of cancer I had. We talked for about forty-five minutes. We talked about fears and how unlucky we were to get a cancer that predominately occurs in heavy smokers and heavy drinkers. We were neither.

His mom's eyes mirrored the look I saw in my wife's eyes. Mothers are used to nurturing and caring for their families, allaying fears and fixing problems. But there was no simple Band-Aid to the invasive enemy—it permeates the well and renders even the strong helpless. Cancer is a scary word and for good reason. The woman's son was in cancer's clutches, and it was apparent that she did not know what to do.

I could see he was getting tired. This was his first foray from Middle Earth; I recalled my first journey and how difficult it had been. The man and his mother were extremely pleased I had taken the time to say hello. The meeting was therapeutic for me as well. It was nice to meet someone from Middle Earth on the surface, exchanging stories of fear and hope.

I can't begin to describe what I knew it took for this gentleman to get dressed, get into a car, and venture out into the public's eye. The physical energy is one aspect, but the emotional energy and courage involved in making it to the coffee shop is quite another thing. Sitting there with his mother, he watched people go about their daily tasks, happy and seemingly without a worry. The two of them were stranded on an island in the local Starbucks, and I joined them for a brief time. It is very lonely being sick.

It struck me that this random act of kindness paid huge dividends for both the giver and the receiver. My understanding of service was deepening. The medical treatment I received was amazing, but it was the countless kindnesses from family, friends, hospital staff, volunteers, and strangers that added incredible therapeutic value. I know this because all these things—a smile, words of encouragement, a helping hand— reinforced my will and remain a part of me today. Cost of a simple act of kindness—priceless!

Oh mercy, mercy me,
Things ain't what the used to be
~Marvin Gaye

15

Lottery Ticket

Throughout different times of the year, most major cancer hospitals run a lottery. Monies are raised through these lotteries to aid in research.

I was in the lobby of the Princess Margaret Hospital (PMH) in Toronto, one of the premier cancer hospitals in North America. They have a kiosk set up in the lobby of the hospital selling hospital lottery tickets. The tickets are a hundred dollars each. Before I contracted cancer, I had always purchased a ticket because it supported a great cause—and also the odds were pretty good for a lottery!

When I had been diagnosed with the first cancer, I had figured it was my time to win. Five years passed without a win of any sort, not even a gym bag! After I was diagnosed with the second cancer, I thought this was my time to win a prize—illogical thinking at its best! But, hey, my sense of entitlement was real and, bizarrely, tangible.

I was expressing that sentiment to the volunteer selling the tickets. Other people were gathered around the booth filling out the required form. I noticed a gentleman standing beside me with a white cane. I told him I was going to win the big prize this time, and it would not be worth his while buying a ticket. Trash talking can become an art form, and I was ready to box this guy out.

The man was blind, and he told me a story about his experience with the CNIB (Canadian National Institute for the Blind) lottery. He had just recently gone blind because of a cancer and was having a tough time adjusting to his new life. So, like me with the cancer lottery, he figured he was sure to win in the CNIB lottery. He told me and the few people that had gathered around the kiosk that he indeed had won something from the CNIB lottery. We were so happy for him, so I asked him what he had won. When he told us what he had won, we couldn't stop laughing. He had won a pair of high-powered binoculars!

I have thought about that chance encounter many times. All of us were fighting our own battles, but to come together and have a laugh made the day for all of us. We wished each other good luck and good health and left the lobby of Princess Margaret with smiles on our face. Winning the lottery has taken on a new meaning for me since that beautiful day.

Life's like a road you travel on. When there's one day here, and the next day gone. Sometimes you bend, sometimes you stand. Sometimes you turn your back to the wind.
~Rascal Flatts

16

Heading to Middle Earth Once Again

Having been through one cancer, I was very aware of keeping on top of screening for other cancers. One statistic that was etched into my brain was that people who have had a cancer are more susceptible to having another cancer. Fact. Not fair, but a fact. In 2002, at age forty-seven, I had my PSA taken along with a digital exam. My PSA was 2.0. PSA is a simple blood test used to screen for prostate cancer. PSA stands for prostate specific antigen. PSA is a protein that is produced by cancerous or non-cancerous tissue in the prostate gland. My physician at the time noted that my prostate felt a little enlarged and rough. He suggested that we keep a close eye on the PSA over the next year. Looking back, I should have requested a biopsy at that time.

In the spring of 2004, my PSA had increased to 3.5. In the fall of 2004, I went back to my family physician. He said the blood test had revealed a PSA of 5.5. He said we should keep an eye on it and asked me to book an appointment six months down the road. I suggested to him that I thought I should have biopsy. He didn't agree with me, and we had a bit of a stand-off. I said with my past history, I would really like to have a biopsy. In fact, I told him I was not leaving his office without a requisition to a urologist to have my prostate biopsied. I am usually not that assertive in situations like that, but in this case, it was my health, and I had to be the number one advocate to help me stay alive. I don't mean to bore you with numbers that probably don't mean anything to the general public. However, if there are middle-aged men reading this, perhaps these few paragraphs will inspire them to get screened for prostate cancer. One other thing: always trust your gut instinct when it concerns your own body. The biopsy was taken on December 13, 2004.

Before the biopsy, the doctor explained to me that, with the PSA score and the roughness of the gland, he felt there was a 50/50 chance that it was cancerous. This was December 13, 2004. I would not get the results of the biopsy until January 5, 2005. During the holidays, I was preoccupied waiting for the results. History was repeating itself, but surely the news this time would be different. The situation did increase my awareness of every little thing during the holidays.

During the hour-and-a-half drive to the doctor on January 5, I played out both scenarios in my mind of how I was going to react to the news. I again thought of myself driving home with the music cranked, on top of the world and not the victim. The next instant, my mind would play out the negative scenario. How would the family cope with me being sick again? Could I cope with being sick again? I tried to focus on the positive outcome, but the negative thoughts kept overriding it. My mind wouldn't cooperate; I kept worrying the festering wound of dread until it bled. I just wanted to get the results. A month of uncertainty was coming to an end.

The news was once again not good: I had prostate cancer. It was a very aggressive and fast growing cancer. The only option was removal of the prostate gland. The next three weeks were once again filled with appointments for blood work, CT Scans, MRI's, and X-rays. I was better prepared in one sense, but my knowledge of what lay ahead also exacerbated my fears.

Surgery was booked for Wednesday, January 25. January hasn't been a good month for me—my other cancer was diagnosed on January 20. It's funny how you remember these dates.

Wednesday, January 25, a typical surgery day: arrive three hours early and move from the outside waiting room to the inside waiting room. Getting ready for any operation is stressful. The one to remove my prostate was going to be major. I was tense to say the least; I knew I wouldn't be the same man as I was before. The doctor told me there would be three hurdles to face. First, the main goal would be staying alive; in other words, I needed to have everything necessary to eradicate the cancer. The second hurdle would be incontinence. The third hurdle might be impotence, not importance. I was only worried about staying alive at this point. I would deal with the other concerns; staying alive trumped everything. The operation was performed by Dr. Short.

When we arrived at the hospital, I went to the admitting department. Before long, I was sitting in a waiting room with one of those beautiful hospital gowns on. Being six foot five, these gowns never quite fit me. I didn't care; my modelling days were over! It's quite a fashion show in the inside waiting room. Everyone is sitting with their legs crossed, wearing designer paper slippers. There is not a single entity on this earth that transcends culture, race, and status in society, as much as wearing a hospital gown. A CEO of a major corporation can walk into a hospital with designer shoes, wearing an impeccably pressed shirt and tie, exuding confidence but is stripped of all this once he puts on a hospital gown. Here the CEO is just like everyone else in the waiting room. Little does he know I am just a simple teacher, yet we are both dressed the same, most likely dealing with something that we hadn't planned on dealing with. It wasn't on our calendar to get sick. I had mentioned PTSD a few chapters ago. Every time I put on a hospital gown, and there has been so many times, my body reacts in a way that doesn't seem familiar. I know my heart rate and blood pressure go through the roof as I think of the previous times I have worn the gowns. I'm not sure if it is PTSD, but something is throwing off my sense of well-being when I put on a gown. One thing I know for sure is that I will never dress up for Hallowe'en wearing scrubs! There is a lot of anxiety on the faces of the people waiting. I was also very weak from not eating and having to clean my plumbing out the day before. I looked around the waiting room and wondered what the other people were having done to their bodies. To ease the tension, my wife and I started up conversations with the others in the waiting room. We all had the same feeling of uneasiness and uncertainty. Once the silence was broken, a listener from the outside waiting room would think there was a party going on behind the closed door.

My name was called. My real name is Earl Martin McCrone. That's our little secret. It always takes me a while to respond, as I think they are calling my dad. Early on in my journeys into hospitals, I would always correct the person calling my name and say, "My real name is Earl, but I go by Marty." After a while I decided, "You know what? There's nothing wrong with the name Earl." You don't hear it very often. I think it was my redneck side of me coming out wanting to be called Earl. The Dixie Chicks paid homage to the name Earl in their song "Goodbye Earl." I wish my name was being called for winning a lottery, not to summon me to an operating room. I kissed my wife goodbye, and off I went down the hall, feeling a humbling, disarming, cool breeze under my gown! My heart rate and blood pressure immediately increased. This was the end of my body functioning the way I was used to and the beginning of another era…another scar, more side effects to deal with, both short term and long term. I had my game face on. It didn't matter how different I was going to be after the operation, they were going to take out the cancerous prostate gland, and I was going to beat the cancer.

While lying on the cold stainless steel operating table, my mind started to wander. In any stressful situation, I try to find a humorous side to the situation. The operating room was busy with the nursing staff prepping for the operation. The lights were bright, and the table and room were cold. A nurse went over my personal information to confirm that I was, in fact, the correct patient for the planned operation. As she was nearing the end of a list of questions, I interrupted her to say that I wanted to clarify with them that I was here for a penis enlargement! The entire operating room laughed! A nurse out of my sight replied, "Not with a doctor named Short!" What a great comeback! I then asked if there was a Doctor Long in the building. More laughs, but then reality hit. The doctor arrived, and we chatted briefly. The anesthetist hooked me up, and after a few questions, I was asleep. I always try to see how long I can stay awake. It's the competitor in me. But I know when I wake up, I will be dealing with the side effects of the anesthetic and the operation. The next thing I knew, I was waking up in the recovery room.

When I awoke, my wife Julie was at my side. We had been down this road before. I still say it is far easier being the patient than the caregiver. The operation was five hours. That is a long time for someone to wait. I had it easy; I was unconscious. She is my gift.

I had a catheter running out of my penis attached to a urine bag. During my five-day stay in the hospital, the amazing nurses showed me how to change from the day urine bag to the night bag. Near the end of the stay, I would go for a short walk with the IV stand. It was uncomfortable with the catheter attached and the stitches in my stomach. Even though I was on a morphine drip, I remember everyone who visited, and although I wasn't a ball of fire, I really enjoyed those visits.

After five days, I was discharged. The catheter would stay attached for another ten days. Those were ten uncomfortable days. Sleeping was difficult because every time I moved the catheter would pull. That sure got my attention in a hurry! I was on a codeine-based painkiller, which made it extremely difficult to have a bowel movement. After five days without a bowel movement, a nurse specializing in enemas arrived. Boy, was I glad to see her. That was a great day in a primal kind of way. It's funny how the description of a great day changes when you're in the cancer game. The catheter, along with the trauma to the area, made it extremely difficult to sit. A cushioned doughnut ring made sitting bearable. Once I found a comfortable position, I would not want to move. Many times I would be out for a drive in the car and get into a comfortable position. I would drive all around town not wanting to go home as that meant changing positions. There were times when I would drive to the lakefront and sleep in the car. Those were excellent power naps.

Despite having bad expectations about the catheter's removal, it was a piece of cake. However, life after the catheter was frustrating. Even though I had religiously exercised the muscles surrounding the bladder (Kegel exercises), I had no control of my urine flow—it was the beginning of months in diapers. I have to say I am now an expert in adult diapers. I could call them other names, but in reality they are diapers…and they do work. Going to the checkout at the pharmacy with a couple of packages of diapers was quite an experience.

Over the next two months, I went from using eight to ten diapers a day to just a few per day. Eventually one diaper would last all day.

In April, I met with the radiation oncologist. Because my cancer had a Gleason score of eight and I was relatively young, I was faced with a decision: would I elect not to have radiation and keep an eye on my PSA score, or would I have radiation therapy now and get it out of the way? A Gleason score is on a scale of ten. A high score marks a fast growing cancer. It is not a good thing to have a Gleason score of eight or above. With the first choice, if my PSA started to increase, I would have to have radiation therapy at that time. I elected to have radiation therapy as soon as possible.

I was in crisis mode, and I wanted to do everything I could to eradicate the cancer.

So here I go once again. Thirty-three trips to Princess Margaret Hospital (sixty miles one way). My first appointment was at the end of June in 2005. I was recovering in Florida at the time, so I had to make my way back for the treatments. Actually, the entire family was in Florida. Julie and Jake would be coming back to Canada a few days after me, and Luke would return with me. My first radiation appointment was scheduled late in the day. In the morning, Luke and I left Florida with our two dogs to fly into Toronto. We arrived at the Toronto airport with two bags of luggage each, accompanied with each dog and it's respective cage. How is that for keeping your mind off of the upcoming treatment? We made our way through the airport and onto the shuttle bus to take us to our car. The day was extremely hot and humid. Luke had never been to Princess Margaret Hospital because he had been in Baltimore when I was undergoing treatment back in 2000. We made it down to the hospital, gave the dogs a good walk, and then headed inside for treatment. We parked in an underground parking garage, which luckily was cool enough to leave the dogs in the car. I remember saying to Luke that someday this hospital would be turned into a condominium and stories would be told of how it used to be a place where people came for treatment for a disease called cancer. That was a very special day for Luke and me.

The remaining thirty-two trips, Julie drove me to the hospital. Most days, we would leave at six in the morning and be home before noon. During the two cancers, I had travelled 13,000 kilometres and spent approximately 240 hours in the car just for radiation treatments. That doesn't include all the trips before the treatments began and after they were over. From my hometown of Barrie, Ontario, that equates to five-and-a-half trips to Disneyworld in Orlando, Florida. If only I had covered all that distance to see Mickey and Goofy rather than to be zapped with radiation. There were days when the radiation machine would have broken down, and we would be there all day. But that was okay because we were together. The radiation to the prostate area was a lot easier than the radiation in the head and neck area. There were, however, unpleasant side effects throughout and after the radiation. As the weeks progressed, I became increasingly tired. There was burning of the skin in the affected area. A cream provided a little relief.

Once again, I was in diapers as the radiation decreased the control of urine flow. I had now cleared the first hurdle that the doctor had explained to me—staying alive. I had done everything possible to eradicate the cancer. I could do no more.

My body should glow with all the radiation I have received. So how did I, someone who had never broken a bone, never spent a day in the hospital, cope with being radiated a total of fifty-eight times along with undergoing two major surgeries?

Whether you're a brother or whether
you're a mother
You're stayin' alive, stayin' alive"
~Bee Gees

17

Definitions

Having an illness seemed to make me consider how I defined myself. Does the *What you do* become the *Who you are*? Are roles definitive in and of themselves? So, athlete, husband, teacher, father, coach—does that say who I am? When I was diagnosed, I saw my definition disappear, and I became another cancer story—a story for others to talk about, pity, and feel glad it wasn't their own story.

A close friend of mine had lost her hair during chemotherapy. Her pallor was noticeable and immediately identifiable to all of us who have dwelt in Middle Earth. One day at lunch, she became irritated with feeling overheated and having a wig on. Julie said to her, "Who cares? Just take it off!" When our friend did, another woman came over and congratulated her for her courage to be in public while fighting cancer. Our friend considered this and after the woman left, quietly stated, "I am more than just this cancer. I am still a weaver, a wife, a mother, a teacher—that's who I want you to see!"

I have often thought of this when I consider definitions. Probably one of the harder cancers to experience, in terms of definitions, is the prostate cancer. So much of the male identity is wrapped up in the attributes that govern our sexuality. Understanding the disease, treatment, and the temporary but still demeaning process of recovery, I reached a plateau of understanding my new physical reality. It has not been an easy acceptance as it involves a deeper, private definition of me. The male psyche has some commonly shared characteristics, but every man individualizes and personalizes that psyche as he undergoes his own life's experiences. I still have a long way to go before I am at peace with all the psychic changes, but in the meantime, my fallback is always the gifts from Julie and my sons— unconditional love and humour.

After recovering from prostate surgery and radiation, I was at a local Starbucks, waiting for two friends to show up for a coffee. I was able to secure three soft, comfortable chairs. The "boys" showed up, and we all ordered our drinks. We looked good, as good as any three fifty-year-olds could. It suddenly occurred to me that we were a unique threesome. One of these friends had had testicular cancer and is missing a testicle. The other friend had had colo-rectal cancer and has a colostomy bag. And of course, I had had prostate cancer. In the middle of the conversation, I realized that if any of us were to go on a date, all of us would have to go along. I said to the boys that it would take all three of us to make one man. Well, we laughed and laughed. Every time I pass those easy chairs, I smile.

Anyone who passed us by would have had no idea of the ordeal all three of us had had to endure. More importantly, we each were still who we were. Cancer would not define us.

Every new beginning comes from
some other beginning's end.
~Semisonic

18

Diapers

Diapers at fifty! Are you kidding me? I don't think so…Well the diaper phase of my recovery was not a lot of fun, but like anything else, you get used to it. They can be called a lot of other names, but the bottom line is, I was wearing diapers. That period of time for me lasted from January to August. Let me tell you, summer was not a time to be wearing diapers. Wearing them was one thing, but buying them was another story.

I am not sure which was harder to buy—condoms when you were younger or diapers when you are older. It's pretty hard to hide a package of diapers at the checkout counter! I did become somewhat of an expert on which ones fit the best and when they were on sale. How many people get the Wednesday or Friday flyer and look to see who has the best deal on adult diapers? I was now that guy…geez, Louise!

I tended to purchase them from the same few stores, and it seemed the same person was always on the cash. In the beginning, I told the girl the diapers were for my dad. On subsequent visits to the store, she would ask how my dad was making out. I felt bad because we had developed a relationship, and she was taking an interest in my life. My little white lie was getting more complicated. What was I to do? I bailed out and drove across town to another store in the same chain to avoid any embarrassment. This reminds me of a time when I was caught in another little white lie. Actually it wasn't me, it was my friend who set me up. Wayne Gretzky had just opened his new restaurant downtown Toronto. In the beginning of the restaurant, a lot of celebrities would dine at his restaurant. Julie and I met with another couple at Gretzky's for dinner. At that time, my hair was longer at the back. Not quite a mullet, but closing in on one. Some people thought I was Richard Dean Anderson. He was the actor who starred in *MacGyver*. So here we were having a nice dinner, and the waitress came up and asked if I was Richard Dean Anderson. I was just about to say no when my friend said, "I knew somebody would recognize you." Before I could say anything, she asked if she could have a picture with me—she had a camera in her locker. My friend answered her and said, "Sure." I was dying now. How was I going to get out of this? Of course, my friend took it to the next level and said to the server, "You can have his picture if you will get Gretzky to have a picture with us." Gretzky and his dad were a few tables over from ours. Over she went to ask Gretzky. Gretzky looked over and laughingly told her that I was not Richard Dean Anderson. She came back to our table, and we could see what had transpired. We knew that we were caught in a tangled web and that Wayne and his dad thought it was hysterical. My friend did the right thing and explained it was all his fault. She took it well, and we all had a great laugh. And yes, we did have a picture taken together.

After a while, I was feeling better and realized I wouldn't have to wear these things for much longer. I also realized that I was in control of my feelings. If I felt humiliated, I was doing that to myself. At the end of the spring, our boys returned from university. I was thrilled to have them home, but I didn't want to see "that look." Cancer had hit once before, and the boys had been through a lot. On good days, I would rationalize that my experience with cancer helped make the boys who they were—understanding, empathetic, and not taking anything in life for granted. On bad days, my egotistical and judgmental self blamed me for putting my sons through a hellish journey to Middle Earth. We all had climbed back together.

Now the boys were home, and I knew there would be some point when they'd walk in and see me dressing or undressing with my diapers on. Of course, this situation cropped up almost immediately. My younger son, Jake, came in talking about a movie he'd like to see and stopped midstream as I stood by my bureau, dressed only in my Depends. So I looked at him and said, "You've been a bad boy!" and proceeded to spank myself while prancing around the room on my toes! We both went into hysterical laughter, bringing Luke and Julie into the scene. All of us recall that moment at different times—we still laugh, and they still care.

Winter, spring, summer or fall
All you have to do is call
And I'll be there
You've got a friend
~Carol King

19

Friends

When I became ill, it was very interesting how friends reacted. In talking with people who have had cancer, they tend to say the same thing. Most have been surprised how their family, friends, workplace companions, and fellow church members rally and give support. In general, people love to help those in need. There are, however, family and friends who disappear and lend no support whatsoever.

I remember being in a coffee shop shortly after radiation and surgery, down sixty pounds, clothes hanging off me, and looking quite hideous thanks to the stitches and staples in my neck. Across the coffee shop, sat a couple with whom Julie and I had been quite close. The couple gave a sheepish wave and went back to their conversation. Julie and I were both stunned. Since this was our first attempt at going out in public, we had just wanted some form of normalcy. What just happened? Did we do something wrong? What were they saying by their aloofness? Julie immediately morphed into her mama bear mode and became protective, saying, "This is their problem to deal with, not yours. Some people are just uncomfortable around illness or feel their own mortality." We left the coffee shop feeling terrible. They had treated us like I wasn't supposed to be back in the Land of the Well. These friends made me feel invisible and alone. Had I listened more closely to mama bear, I would have found the deeper meaning, that it was entirely our friends' issue. Their inability to deal with my state at that moment took me away from my joy—coffee with my wife. I was distracted from the lesson my friend with brain cancer had taught me—live in the moment, start enjoying the small stuff.

Now, being a great guy, I got cancer a second time, so that some of these family and friends who had vanished could have a chance to redeem themselves. Again, some stepped up while others repeated the vanishing act. I am pleased to report that the couple in the coffee shop went overboard to be supportive during my second cancer. Such a prince am I, giving them a second chance.

I've thought about people's reactions to my cancers and realized these same reactions apply to many crises in people's lives like loss of a job, divorce, retirement, and accidents. It seems that the focus is misplaced. I found out later that the people who had felt reluctant about coming to see me had obsessed about what they should say. However, it's not what they ended up saying to me that was important, it was their presence that I valued and remembered. I SEE YOU!

When I was in the hospital for five weeks and on morphine, I couldn't recall any conversation I had with visitors, but I could remember who was there and where they sat. That was the single most important thing because they did see me and give me a sense of belonging. Being there as a friend or family member helped me climb out of Middle Earth. It may seem like a small thing, but to me, it was a major step in the right direction. Every visit or conversation took me a little closer to the Land of the Living as I paddled through the narrows.

I knew when I was in the hospital that life would never be the same because of my experiences, but there is no question that the process of embracing a new and healthier identity takes time. That is why being connected to those I'd befriended and loved became vitally important. I needed to feel that I had the support and encouragement of family and friends.

A friend from elementary school visited me in the hospital. I hadn't seen him in fifteen years. I haven't seen him since, but I do remember that he was there. He helped me get closer to the surface and back to the Land of the Living. I will always be grateful to him. Small kindnesses have more value than I'd ever realized.

When the night has come
And the land is dark
And the moon, is the only, light we'll see
No I won't, be afraid
No I won't, be afraid
Just as long, as you stand, stand by me
~Ben E King

20

What Was I Thinking?

We always had a dog when I was growing up. When we were first married, our gift and honeymoon to each other was going to get a yellow-lab puppy. At the time of this writing, Julie and I have never been away alone together. We have been married for twenty-six years. How bad is that? We had a trip planned back in 1989, but our younger son had developed a hernia. How many two-year-olds do you hear having a hernia? No regrets, though, through the years. Anytime we have been away, it has been with the boys.

Julie had never had a dog, so the yellow lab was very special for her. Unfortunately, she didn't realize that her allergies would trigger an asthmatic response. After seven years of trying different things, and Julie spending an average of one month in bed each year, it became apparent we'd have to give our beloved dog up. The boys were two and five years old when we let our dog go to live on a friend's farm. It was a heartbreaking decision.

After a move to Baltimore from Barrie, Ontario, Julie and I decided we needed to get another dog, a hypoallergenic one. Our younger son would watch *Animal Planet* relentlessly and badly wanted a dog. The boys had only faint memories of our lab but were dying for a dog to be part of their young lives. One of the main reasons we decided to go ahead and get another dog was to put a positive spin on life and get the attention off the cancer and me. We had a few hypoallergenic breeds to choose from and also wanted a larger dog, so the boys could wrestle with it. I couldn't see six foot six and six foot three boys playing with a small dog. We ended up getting a black standard poodle. We eventually found a husband and wife who had a small operation out of their house. Julie and I went to their place and picked out the dog.

A few weeks later, on a sunny cool October day, we were out in the car, and we said to the boys that we had to stop at a house where a friend of Mom's (Julie) lived. The boys came into the house and discovered lots of eight-week-old puppies. Man, were they cute! I picked up the one we had chosen and put it in Jake's arms. Both boys were over the top with excitement! We asked the boys if they thought it would be neat if we could take this guy home with us. They thought we were kidding. When they realized we were serious, they were the happiest guys on the planet! At that particular moment, they had totally forgotten about Dad and his cancer. From now on, the centre of attention was "Murray."

A funny dynamic began. Even though Julie and I had based our decision to get a dog on the boys and how they could move forward and away from sweating the big stuff, I began to gain huge dividends from this little puppy myself. Luke and Jake would head out every day with Julie—the boys would be going to school and Julie to work. I was alone in a new city, in a condo with nothing but the aftermath of cancer treatment looming all around me. The depression was real, the gloom was oppressive, and I was cut off from the support of family and friends. I would spend my days watching the Biography Channel and watching a show called *Whatever Happened to...*I soon realized I was spending my days watching other people's lives and it was time to get on with my own. I wondered, "Whatever happened to Marty McCrone?" This tiny black ball of fur came into my life and slowly gave me meaning. I had to think about somebody else; I had to go outside—several times a day—and I had to start training Murray. Slowly but surely, I could feel myself wanting to do things. I would also catch myself talking away to Murray and sharing many things with him. While I laughed and cried my way through these discussions, I believed Murray understood. Sometimes I shared thoughts and fears with Murray that I hadn't shared with anyone. And to Murray's credit, he never told anyone. Murray was a great listener.

Fast forward five years to my diagnosis with another cancer. I was scheduled to have my cancerous prostate gland removed at the end of January. At this time in our life, Julie and Jake were living in Orlando where Julie was teaching at Lake Highland Prep, and Jake was in his senior year at that school. I was back in Ontario teaching and commuting to Orlando every four weeks or so. It wasn't ideal, but it was best for our son. Julie took two weeks off and came up to Ontario to be with me for the operation. At her private school, you only got a few days off a year—the rest of her team gave her some of their days off, so that she could be here for the two weeks. What wonderful people!

Prior to the operation, I started thinking of another dog. We had seen a relatively new breed of dog called a golden doodle. It was hypoallergenic and large. To keep my mind off the surgery, I spent a lot of time researching the dog and finding a breeder that had a litter ready to go. Three days after coming home from the hospital, Julie and I drove an hour and a half to just look at the dog. You know what happened next. Nobody goes and just looks at a dog and comes back empty-handed! If you're lucky, you leave with just one dog. Was I losing it? What was I thinking? This was a Saturday and Julie was going back to Orlando on Sunday. I still had my catheter in, and it would stay in for another week or so. I would be all alone with an eight-week-old puppy! Murray, our other dog, was in Orlando at this time. How would I manage? It is hard enough training a puppy when you are a hundred percent, let alone recovering from a major operation.

We called our golden doodle "Fozzie Bear." Fozzie sped up my recovery like Murray had five years before. If Fozzie hadn't been there, I would have spent the next few months in bed. There would have been no reason to get up and get going. The Fozman made sure I was up—all the time!

I was always told that a good puppy is a tired puppy. I took Fozzie for long walks, sometimes in thigh-deep snow to tire him out. When Foz would sleep in the afternoon, I would grab a power nap. The sound of him going down on the floor to sleep was music to my ears…but, unfortunately, just as spontaneously, Fozzie Bear would be up, raring to go.

It was February, and it was cold and snowy. After a full day of trying to tire the Foz out with long walks, it was time to go to bed. Bedtime was always a matter of trying to find a comfortable position so the catheter wouldn't be pulled. The catheter was hooked up to a large bag at night, which would collect urine. This bag would rest on the floor beside the bed. I couldn't believe how much urine was produced throughout the night. This is the kind of information I never needed to know. One night, Foz was sleeping on his dog bed beside my bed, and I managed to find a comfortable position as I drifted off to sleep. I was quite proud of myself for getting through the day with such a young dog.

At three o'clock in the morning, I awakened to Fozzie crying. He needed to go outside and do his business. I tried negotiating with him to buy a few more hours of sleep. I was so comfortable in bed, the catheter was not pulling, and it was cold and snowy outside. However, my negotiating skills failed miserably; he just didn't get it! I had no choice but to get out of bed and take him outside.

I manoeuvred to the side of the bed trying to not let the catheter pull. (I keep referring to the catheter even though, once you've had the experience, even the word "catheter" causes an involuntary muscle spasm, at least in me.) I got to the side of the bed and put on my slippers. I then reached down and grabbed the nighttime urine bag; it must have weighed five pounds. I was wearing a T-shirt and slippers—that's all. I then reached down and picked up Fozzie. Bear in mind, reaching down to the floor wasn't one of the preferred movements in this condition. I then had to make my way down a flight of stairs. Picture this—a dog in one hand, urine bag in the other, holding onto the railing as I descended the stairway with slippers that tended to fall off. I called this, "Doing the urine bag shuffle." That was the easy part of the journey. I increased the speed of the shuffle because I didn't know how long the Foz could hold out. I made it to the door. I couldn't let the dog down on the floor, as I was afraid he would do his business right there and then. The side door is a little tricky to open with two free hands, let alone hands occupied by a dog and a full urine bag. Success! The door opened, and we were heading outside to the patio area. More stairs, this time snow covered and slippery. The wind was howling and blowing the snow all around. I threw Fozzie into a snow bank and made my way down the stairs without incident. So here I was standing in a snow storm, at three in the morning, with a T-shirt and slippers on, holding a five pound bag of urine, waiting for the dog to relieve himself. I vividly remembered the fellow I had seen out of my hospital room that rainy evening in April waiting for his dog to go. Man, he was impatient. I wonder how he would have reacted if he had been standing, as I was, in the bitter cold with nothing on but slippers and a shirt. Again, it's all how I choose to frame life and its experiences along the way. I looked up into the sky and laughed: true, deep, resonating belly laughs. I cherished that moment.

What a picture that would have made! Never in my wildest dreams did I ever think I would have an experience like this.

I realize not all people are into dogs or pets in general. For me, having a pet to care for, to train, and to love is the best thing I could have done. It enabled me to creep out of Middle Earth perhaps earlier than I would have. A person's journey through a crisis, through the narrows, leaves valuable lessons in its wake that have helped the transition into new beginnings. I have had two cancers and now have two dogs. I'm not planning on any more dogs—or any more cancers!

When I take Murray and Fozzie Bear for long walks, and it starts to rain, I enjoy the time in the rain because I will never forget the time when I couldn't take such walks. Life is good! I am grateful. I have learned many wonderful lessons.

Oh, put me in coach,
I'm ready to play today
Put me in coach,
I'm ready to play today
Look at me, I can be centerfield
~John Fogerty

21

John

The air was mild for a mid-October night. A dense fog accompanied the steady downpour. The trip down the highway seemed otherworldly. My anguish was mirrored in the rain running down the windshield. I was on my way to visit my university basketball coach who would not be leaving the hospital. John McManus coached me in the 1979–80 season when I attended the Faculty of Education, University of Toronto. Seven other teammates were making the journey as well, coming from all parts of the province.

The man who had brought us all together in 1979 was lying in a hospital room, losing his final battle to cancer. The windshield wipers rhythmically swept from side to side, erasing years and sending me back to the good old days. Coach was an amazing man's man who appealed to all the players because of his one-liners and competitiveness. Crewcut, wearing a short-sleeved white shirt with dress pants, Coach would walk around the gym making consecutive baskets and say, "No rim, boys—no rim! Nothing but net!" I remember at halftime during games, he would give us crap for not playing well. The terms he would use would have us in stitches. He would say, "You're running around like a fart in a mitt," amongst many other sayings.

I parked the car, unsure that I wanted to see Coach like this. My teammates met in the lobby, and we went up to the ICU. Coach was hooked up to some monitors and looked like he was dozing. When he heard one of us say, "Hey Coach!" he opened his eyes and the brightness of recognition shone out.

He was eight-eight years young. Coach would hold court in this tiny hospital room for the next hour. All visitor rules were ignored as he had a way with the nurses. John was full of life; he had the entire room in gales of laughter. It was like a scene out of a movie. Here we were, twenty-five years later, listening to and respecting our coach as we had done long ago. At that moment in time, we were all back in our early twenties, waiting to hear about our next play, admiration and love in all our eyes.

John was old school, and physical activity was still a part of his daily routine; even in the hospital, he did push ups at the end of his bed, followed by long walks around the corridors. The nurses couldn't keep him down!

It was very hard for us to leave and say our last goodbyes to John. We all had a chance for an individual goodbye to Coach. He knew he would not see us again. My last look back into the room as I was leaving will forever be etched in my mind. His look was one of, "It's going to be okay." John passed away two weeks later.

I'd like to think he went out shooting baskets in his mind, hearing the roar of the crowd, and feeling the adoration of his players. When someone elderly passes away, a phrase you will often hear is, "Well he lived a long life." That may be true, but in most cases, the person would love to live one more day. I know John would have—and just as importantly, anyone he touched wanted just one more day with Coach.

What becomes of the broken-hearted
Who had love that's now departed?
I know I've got to find
Some kind of peace of mind
Maybe
~Jimmy Ruffin

22

Diamond Girl

Once I arrived back on the surface of the Land of the Well, there were constant reminders of the days in Middle Earth. Our close friend, Joan, was re-diagnosed with breast cancer ten days after I had been diagnosed with squamous cell cancer. She had been clear of the disease for ten years. This was not an experience I would wish on anyone, and to have someone so dear to us be diagnosed in tandem with me doubled the shock value. Joan, however, was optimistic about our ability to win against this formidable foe and decided that we would gain from each other's strength.

We decided to meet regularly in the lobby of Princess Margaret Hospital in Toronto, as we were both going to be there at the same time for treatments. We agreed on a time, day, and place—the coffee shop in PMH, every Tuesday, at eleven in the morning. If either of us couldn't make it, we would just carry on and meet the following week. As treatment proceeded for both of us, our frailty grew; Joan often had to stay with relatives in Toronto as the two-hour commute from home would have been difficult. Near the end of my treatment regime, I had lost sixty pounds and finally was hospitalized as I was unable to swallow. From a suburban hospital, I took an hour cab ride to and from PMH for the five remaining radiation treatments. It was all I could do to not throw up on the ride. When I am a hundred percent healthy, I cannot stand sitting in the backseat of a car. When I was younger, I would sit in the backseat of the family car. My father would light up a big cigar with all the windows rolled up with the exception of his window, which was open a crack. Hey, maybe that's how I got cancer! So here I am in the back of this smelly taxi cab with literally no suspension left in the car, cold and damp, driving along a rough highway trying to not vomit in the cab. I travelled with a vomit bag, and I threw up four out of the five rides. The taxi driver did not look like a happy camper. Can't blame him. I can just imagine his conversation around the dinner table that night. At least I gave him something to talk about with his family. I never had the same driver on the way home back to the hospital. I would have to wait for the cab to arrive which wasn't a lot of fun when you're down sixty pounds, freezing cold all the time, and nauseated.

Even though this period of time would often be a blur to me, partly because of my condition, and partly because of the morphine I was on, I can vividly remember looking forward just to seeing Joan. If it was for a short while, hugs and words of comfort before rushing to the washroom with nausea, or a long while, full of empathetic chat, some laughter, some tears, I yearned to see Joan. Joan and her husband, Wally, would often be waiting in the same two chairs in the lobby. I didn't know which end was up, but I can tell you about our conversations. More importantly, I can tell you how I felt. Joan, her face, her voice, to this day makes me feel safe, loved, and calm.

She was full of life. One day the phone rang, and Joan wanted to know if we would like to go to a concert in Wasaga Beach on a Saturday night in July. Julie said yes to the concert. I asked who was playing, and she said it was some group called The Funk Brothers. I don't think I'm very good at being receptive to unknown adventures—okay, I'm lousy at it. So, I started to put up all the roadblocks why this wasn't a good idea—the traffic on a Saturday in July to such a popular tourist beach; the unknown group; where to park; the kind of people that might be there; and blah, blah, blah. Julie did what she does best: she nodded sympathetically and continued to plan for the event.

Just to back up a little, Joan was on a two-year regime of chemotherapy. She was moving up the hierarchy of drugs, knowing that, at best, she would be able to contain the cancer and squeeze out some more living. She was weak and frail. I was complaining of having to go to the beach while Joan was kicking my butt as far as being positive and seizing every day and loving life. That was the motivation Julie used; it was like a splash of cold water. Reality at its worst!

A few days before the concert, Joan suggested coming up earlier and doing a picnic on the beach. When my complaining started again, my wife asked me if I wanted to call the "wambulance." It was going to happen—Julie knew it, and I knew it. This was her matron of honour, her best woman, and nothing would stop her from making every effort to be with Joan.

That afternoon and evening in July was one of the most memorable days I will have had. Joan and Julie threw together a picnic that would rival a five-star restaurant. The weather was magnificent, and we were all so happy.

The concert was held right on the beach. The moon was full, glittering on the water like a sea of diamonds. The unknown group turned out to be some incredible studio musicians. The Funk Brother had played on every Motown hit record of the '60s and '70s. They have more number one hits than the Beatles, Rolling Stones, and Elvis combined. Joan Osborne also sang with the Funk Brothers that night, expressing her great admiration and reverence for them.

Julie and Joan got up and danced to the music. Joined by Joan's daughter, Caitlin, they all locked arms and swayed to the music, singing as each song revived a distant memory. To see Julie and Joan laughing, dancing, and singing together was a magical moment. Time stood still, and Joan was allowed to shed the shackles of her debilitating illness, if only for a brief moment. Not long after, Joan's cancer spread to her brain. She died a few months later. That last hooray on the beach was a great tribute to a beautiful person, our "Diamond Girl." It also again left us knowing that life is in the moment, not the future or past.

To this day when I enter the lobby of Princess Margaret Hospital, I look over at the chair where Joan usually sat, and I say hi to her. Near the end of her life, when the cancer had spread to her brain, Joan was confused because of the morphine and the effects of the cancer. She would say to me that she would meet me in the lobby of Princess Margaret Hospital on Tuesday, and we would go for a coffee. I told her I was looking forward to seeing her at the coffee shop and that I would buy. This made her very happy; it made me eternally grateful.

Our meetings in March and April of 2000 had unmistakably had an impact on Joan and me. Even in her final struggle with cancer, she felt strength from our bond. Joan understood her time was limited, but she accepted this with a grace and dignity which in a way made it that much easier for her family and many friends, even as they felt her loss. She died in 2005.

Another friend, Paul, was undergoing treatment at the same time as I was being treated for my second bout with cancer, the prostate cancer. Paul was one of those truly nice guys. He had a way of making everyone feel important. I remember seeing him coming out of a grocery store as I was entering. We stood there for at least a half an hour talking. Again, I remember the uplifting feeling we both felt as we acknowledged the battle. It was therapeutic for both of us. Paul passed away in 2006. Every time I enter that grocery store, I stop and say hi to Paul. Such an insignificant meeting that day will forever be a part of me. Paul lived his life fully, beginning as an elite athlete, then embracing family life, coaching, and teaching. Paul played hockey at the University of Notre Dame. He was a superstar there and had many records that still hold today. When I came back from Baltimore to teach in Ontario, Paul was my vice-principal. Our son Luke was playing basketball for Harvard University. Harvard University was travelling to Notre Dame for a basketball game, so I thought I would drive down with another friend to see the game and visit the University. I picked Paul's brain as to where to stay and where to eat. He was so excited I was going down to his alma mater. I felt I needed to go down a day early. Therefore, I was taking off Friday and leaving early on Thursday. I was trying to keep this whole plan on the down-low, but of course, Paul knew about it. I still remember seeing Paul at the end of a hallway around noon on Thursday. He looked at his watch and said, "Marty what are you still doing here?" As soon as we arrived at Notre Dame, we went directly to the hockey arena to see all the plaques with all different statistics. Man did Paul hold a lot of records. Paul was just one of the nice guys. He was keenly interested in everything around him and always showed great delight as he listened to others. I gained a great deal just by knowing him; it's my obligation to give back to others out of respect for Paul and the example he set.

I have more than just my will to live—I have an urge to live life to the fullest for people like Joan and Paul. Telling about losing two friends to cancer may sound morose. The vitality and positivity they evoked in all who knew them makes theirs, stories of inspiration. They made sure that they enjoyed each moment and they wanted their families and friends to grab life and go all out.

Now when I remember spring
All the joy that love can bring
I will be remembering
The shadow of your smile
~Andy Williams

23

Auntie Ev

I had just completed my course of radiation treatments. As you can imagine, I was in rough shape. It was Luke's birthday, and I suggested to Julie and Jake that they should drive to Baltimore and be there to celebrate his birthday. We worked out a plan where I would stay with my Auntie Ev in Toronto while they were away visiting Luke in Baltimore. You might think that my last sentence was a little crass because I said we would stay with my Auntie Ev. Of course, we would ask her in advance, and we knew the answer would be a resounding yes as it always was. My aunt is one of those rare one-of-a-kind people. To accurately describe Auntie Ev, we have to go back to my childhood. Auntie Ev and Uncle Ed were high school sweethearts. They married young and lived in my uncle's family home their entire life. It was in the east end of Toronto at Jones Avenue and Gerard Street. When our family would visit them on weekends, we would stay overnight. Saturday nights were magical. We would have our pyjamas on while waiting in anticipation for *Hockey Night in Canada* to come on the TV, so we could watch the Toronto Maple Leafs. There were always candies in fancy dishes throughout the house. After dinner, Auntie Ev would sit down with my brother and me and play games with us. It usually started off with Bingo. My aunt would give us pennies—man were we rich! Then we would slide into a game of Snakes and Ladders, followed by Snap or War. As I am writing this, I can hear her soft voice laughing as one of us would hit a snake and go back down the board. It is funny how the brain works. I was just transported back into time in which I was a six-year-old boy playing games with my Auntie Ev. Frank Sinatra could be heard playing on the hi-fi record player, and I could hear laughter in the other room with my father or Uncle Ed telling jokes. When the hockey game started, my brother and I would sit on the floor intently, watching the Maple Leafs, hoping they would score first. It was like something you would see in a commercial with two short-haired blonde boys sitting on the floor in their pyjamas watching *Hockey Night in Canada* on a large cabinet-type television. I realize this was the scene for most people back in the '50s and '60s. Wasn't it a magical time? Also, part of that scene was that you could stay up until the end of the first period, then it was time for bed. My aunt, at the end of the first period, would ask if we would like some cereal before we went to bed. That was a no-brainer because her cereal choices were out of a child's wildest dream. Sugar Pops, Frosted Flakes, Cap'n Crunch, Alpha-Bits, and Rice Krispies. Are you kidding me? To this day, I have cereal every night before I go to bed. And no, they are not the healthiest of choices, but the cereal takes me back to Saturday nights with my aunt and uncle.

So fast forward from a six-year-old boy to a forty-five-year-old bigger boy staying with my aunt once again. My uncle had passed a few years earlier, so my aunt was on her own. The only problem with my stay this time was that it was not long enough. I stayed with her for six days. Those six days, even though I was not feeling that great, were exactly where I needed to be. I always had a choice of about three entrées each night and countless choices of dessert. Of course, cereal was the nightcap every night. Everything had to be soft as my mouth was still reeling from the effects of radiation. Not to be defeated by the hard cereal edges, I let the cereal soak for a while so it would turn almost mushy. Didn't taste as great, but it was still cereal, and I was eating it with my aunt.

Why am I writing a chapter about my aunt? It is simple: she went beyond any expectations to come and see me while I was in the hospital. It took her over two and a half hours to get to the hospital where I was staying. If she had a car, she would've been there in twenty minutes. Buses, street cars, and the subway were her modes of transportation. Guess what she brought me? A couple pairs of nice wool socks and comfortable sweat-pants. To me these were worth a million dollars. Being in the hospital for six weeks my feet and legs were always cold. Auntie Ev didn't have to ask me what I needed. She knew!

Going back a few years, I had just finished university, and I got accepted into the University of Toronto for a Bachelors of Education program. It was pretty cool because I was the first in our extended family to go to University and now teacher's college. My aunt and uncle asked me if I would like to stay with them for the year. Are you kidding me? That was a dream come true. This boy had his aunt and uncle all to himself. On the first day of school, I wandered into the gymnasium to find out when they were going to have tryouts for the basketball team. At this point, I was unsure whether I wanted to play basketball. I just happened to run into the coach, John McManus, and I asked him when they were holding tryouts. He said that night. I hopped on the subway, went back to my aunt and uncle's place, grabbed my basketball gear, and went back to the gymnasium. The reason I mention this is that practices were after school, and most nights I wouldn't get home until 8 p.m. Auntie Ev in her true Aunt Bea tradition would always have my dinner ready for eight, and she would sit and join me for dinner. Our typical routine every night was that we would watch TV shows in the small TV room upstairs. I would always have a school book on my lap as we watched the television. My aunt would ask me, "Don't you need to study?" I always replied that the material in the book would make its way to my brain by travelling through my skin on my lap.

We all have special people in our lives. They shape our lives more than we know. When you are going through difficult times, whether it's sickness, loss of job, divorce, etc., we all handle these challenges differently, but the one common factor in all is how we rely on the positive people we have in our life. Auntie Ev and Uncle Ed were my surrogate parents, with unconditional love, careful listening, and sage advice. Neither of them finished high school, but their wisdom was undeniable. I miss them each and every day.

Appendix A

Bear story

As mentioned earlier, there has only been a small number of adults who have asked "What gotcha?" or "What happened to your neck?" Children, on the other hand, are straight shooters and show no hesitancy in asking what happened to my neck. My business partner and I have run a basketball camp for twenty-seven years. COVID has put a hold on it the last couple of years. We have anywhere from 160 to 180 campers per week. The ages of the campers range from eight to thirteen years of age. The younger children are very curious and would come up to me and ask what happened to my neck. Instead of saying I had cancer, which would be boring to them, I started making up a story of how I was barbecuing my favourite hamburger in the backyard. I set the scene of how our backyard was beside a wooded area. I have bird sounds piped in over the sound system, sounds of a fire crackling, and mosquitos buzzing. I next tell them a storm was moving in, as thunder was rumbling in over the sound system, along with the sound of pouring rain. As the sound of the thunder and rain diminished, I reiterated how this was my favourite burger, and I was going to finish cooking the awesome burger no matter what! Just then over the sound system, rustling grass could be heard. I then asked the campers in a hushed voice if they heard that. Then a loud growl could be heard, then another one. I looked to my right and tell them there was a huge black bear that looked very hungry staring in my eyes. He pawed his way toward the grill and me where that delicious burger was sizzling. It was now a standoff between the bear and me. Before I knew it, the bear had taken a swipe and took half of my neck away. Oh, no! But during this time I never dropped my burger off the spatula. I then grabbed the bear and put him in a bear hold, which seemed appropriate. I said to the bear that swiping my neck wasn't very nice. The bear said he was sorry, so I gave him a hot dog, and he loped back into the woods. As he was fading into the woods, the bear turned to me with a tear in his eye and waved. Now, doesn't that story sound better than just saying I had cancer? Parents would drop their children off the next day and mention the bear story and how remarkable it was that I didn't drop the burger. Lots of early morning laughs!

So here I was, refereeing an elementary tournament for teams in grades four through six. Throughout the game, a little boy kept staring at my neck. He looked like he was in grade four. I knew he wanted to ask what happed to my neck, but even at a young age, he respected my position as a referee and felt he couldn't approach me on the court. As it happened, after the game, we both coincidently left the building at the same time. I said hi to him and started talking about the game. I was in mid-sentence and out came the question. I told him I had a long story about a bear attacking me and a short story about getting cancer, but since I was cut for time, having to get to another game in Barrie, I told him I had cancer. He said, "You had cancer, too?" I laughed all the way to the next game. Don't you love the innocence of kids?

EPILOGUE

Everyone has a story

My goal in writing our family journey was to give insight into how I perceived the experiences that accompanied every aspect of the cancer trip. I wrote about the experience a few years ago. Unfortunately, the journey didn't end there. In fact, unbeknownst to me, it was, in fact, just starting. Dealing with the side effects, (both old and new), of the operations and treatments have been an on-going concern.

A wise man told me years ago, that everyone has a bucket of shit hanging over their head. Throughout your lifetime, the bucket will eventually empty on you. Maybe a little at a time, or perhaps it'll empty all at once, and you say to yourself, "It'll be clear sailing from here on in!" After my first cancer, I was convinced the bucket of shit was empty, and it would indeed be a beautiful vista from here on. I would have no more health problems and life would be hunky-dory. Well, was I ever wrong! It was either a really big bucket, or I had another bucket lined up after the first bucket was empty. The wise man that told me about the theory didn't explain that some buckets are larger than others. And if you're special, like me, you could have a number of buckets of shit hanging over your head ready to drop at any time.

I had mentioned a couple of years ago that when I was thanking everyone for the birthday wishes, I had come down with a new illness. After seeing multiple doctors, I was diagnosed with For Fuck Sakes Syndrome (FFSS). Research has shown there is a direct correlation with the bucket of shit dripping on us, and the number of "for fuck sakes" spoken in a day. My goal is to get down below one hundred for fuck sakes in a day. It's a lofty goal, but being a competitive guy, I'm optimistic I can reach my goal.

I could go on about the side effects, and the trials and tribulations over the past number of years but that is not, and never was, my objective in writing this story. My objective was to give people a little peek into the cancer game and other challenges we face throughout our lifetime.

When I reread the story, I realized how many characters were in our family story—no, actually in our lives: from the young lad in the basement of Princess Margaret Hospital awaiting a new mask to deal with a new cancer; to the gentleman in the coffee shop with his mother, who ventured out of Middle Earth for just a few minutes; to the warriors who come out of their caves to make their way to the lobby of the hospital and hear a song that lets them momentarily escape from Middle Earth. I see in my mind's eye the Middle Earth warriors who are waiting patiently to give blood and then wait. I see the blind fellow buying a lottery ticket, who was dealing with his situation with humour. I see the mechanic, who as of today has been one of just a handful of people who have said, "What gotcha?" And I see our dear Joanie, who danced so carefree under a full moon rising, glimmering against the water on a sand filled beach. To John, my basketball coach who was eighty-eight years young, I'll always remember him doing push-ups at the end of his hospital bed and wanting more days to live.

As well, I hold dear all the people who drove me to the hospital and the friends present in our journey that helped keep a sense of normalcy in our chaotic life. These are real life characters that reached down to Middle Earth and helped with the journey back to the land of the living and healthy.

In writing this epilogue, I started to think of my favourite song "The Weight" by The Band. If the name doesn't ring a bell, I think the chorus will remind you:

Take a load off Fanny
Take a load for free
Take a load off Fanny
And (and) (and) you put the load right on me
(You put the load right on me).

The song is most simply about the burdens we all carry. The weight is the load that we shoulder when we take on responsibility or when we try to do good. There are other meanings to the song, but this meaning really resonates with me. Just as "The Weight" has a cast of characters throughout the song, so does this story, and so does your life. So often we don't see the characters in our life, as well as us, not being seen.

I would like to leave you with this true and inspiring story. A professor, who taught at a university in the United States, held a two-hour class every Thursday in the semester from 2 – 4 p.m. The course he taught was Values and Communications. It was nearing the end of the semester, and the students were busy studying for the final exam. There was so much material to cover. At the end of every class, students would hang out and talk amongst each other and to the professor. When four o'clock hit, a custodian would enter the class and start cleaning the room amongst the students. This was repeated every Thursday in the semester.

Exam day! The students were gathered in groups in the hallway going over last minute information. The door opened to summon the students into the room. With pens in hand, they were ready to give the pens a workout writing the exam. Each desk had an empty booklet in which to answer the questions and an exam booklet.

The exam started, and the students were wishing they had studied enough. As they opened the exam booklet, they realized there was only one question on the exam. Their heads were raised in a questioning manner. As time moved on, the students had become restless in their chairs. The question on the exam read as follows: "In the space provided, write the first name of the custodian who comes into our lecture hall every Thursday at 4 p.m.?"

At the end of the exam, 4 p.m., (yes, every student was instructed to stay until four), the professor collected all ninety exam booklets. The exam results were posted the next day in the hallway. Only one person passed the exam. In other words, out of ninety students in the classroom, only one had made the effort to get to know the custodian. The custodian was invisible to the rest of the class.

As mentioned earlier in the book, just think of how many people we don't see every day. Would you have been the student who passed the course? If not, could you become that person? As the old saying goes, don't judge a book by its cover. Just think how many books we don't open in a day. The fewer the books, the fewer stories you have to tell and reminisce about. Do you want to be known as the bungalow person, having only one story to tell over and over and over again? Why not be the person who initiates conversation, opens the cover of many books, and be the person who is a high-rise with so many stories to their name. I hesitated in writing the last couple of lines because I don't want to sound too preachy. Probably the hardest part of writing these chapters is finding a way to finish the story. I have a missing feeling as I try to come up with a conclusion. Then I thought of listening to the song "The Weight" and how much I enjoy listening to the storyline and all the characters. When it is over, I don't feel sad, as I can replay the song and be with the characters again. I hope you have enjoyed meeting the different characters in my story, and as you go forward, remember them, and add more to your group of characters in your story.

About the Author

Marty teaches at Georgian College, Fitness and Wellness. His passion for teaching and coaching are obvious in his vibrant gym classes. Marty is an advocate for daily quality fitness and wellness and continues to work out. He enjoys walking his dog—in any kind of weather—and actually is returning to skiing. Along with his wife of forty years, Julie, they make their home in Barrie and enjoy golfing in the summer.

Marty can be reached at mmccrone@gmail.com

Manufactured by Amazon.ca
Bolton, ON

33397180R00102